Prais

"...a must read for anyone who has the task of ...
ANNE DAY, FOUNDER, COMPANY OF WOMEN

"Marty Britton's *Screening for the One* offers invaluable insights into navigating today's complex hiring landscape. If you're responsible for building a successful team, this is a must-read."
LISA BRAGG, AUTHOR *BRAGGING RIGHTS: HOW TO TALK ABOUT YOUR WORK USING PURPOSEFUL SELF-PROMOTION*

"...a reassuring and easy-to-digest read by a savvy businesswoman who wants you to succeed."
LIZ RADZICK, PRESIDENT MANIFEST CONSULTING

"...an exceptional look into what it takes to make the right hire."
MARC BELAICHE, COFOUNDER TORONTOJOBS.CA AND GUHUZA.COM

"If you are hiring and want to do it right you MUST READ THIS BOOK!!!!! Thought provoking and informative — Marty knows her stuff!"
JODY STEINHAUER, PRESIDENT & CBO (CHIEF BARGAIN OFFICER) THE BARGAINS GROUP

"Marty's book provides concise, valuable advice, supported by case studies and policies, empowering individuals to make informed decisions. I recommend this book for anyone involved in hiring and managing talent."
JOYCE USHER-MESIANO, VP WESTLAND INSURANCE/WESTLAND MYGROUP

"A must read for anyone wanting to understand the world of pre-employment screening and how the industry helps employers hire the 'RIGHT' candidate."
VIVEK KHANNA, CHIEF CLIENT PARTNER, NEEYAMO INC.

"*Screening for the One* is a call to action for business owners and hiring professionals to take charge of their recruitment processes for significant benefits and minimized risks."
PATRICIA A. MUIR MAESTRO QUALITY INC. (BUSINESS CONSULTANT AND COACH FOR WOMEN-OWNED BUSINESSES)

Marty Britton

Screening for the One

How to Gain an Edge in Your Hiring

Published by Ingenium Books Publishing Inc.
Toronto, Ontario, Canada M6P 1Z2
www.ingeniumbooks.com

ISBNs:
eBook 978-1-990688-36-2
Paperback 978-1-990688-35-5

Edited by Amie McCracken and Linell van Hoepen
Cover Design by Jessica Bell Design via Ingenium Books

To my father, for his entrepreneurial spirit and starting bmp.

To my mother, who started a marketing company in our basement and showed me it was okay to be a mom and have a company she was passionate about.

To my husband, for picking up the slack while I worked insane hours to keep this business going through each economic upheaval.

To my son and daughter, for never making me feel guilty for the hours of work it takes to do what I do.

Contents

Introduction

Being responsible for hiring someone is not an easy job, but it is an important one. A company needs to have great employees if they want to be successful. With the possibility of hundreds of candidates applying for one role, how do you know who will be the best fit?

When you are ready to start interviewing, how do you make a solid, fact-based decision when there are so many variables? Is that person who they say they are? Have they done the things they say they've done? Verifying all of this is a mammoth task, but essential to the hiring process.

How do you know they will work well in your company culture? Will they fit in with their colleagues? Can you be assured they will mesh with their team so they can all work hard and efficiently? Time will tell, of course, but there are also ways of weeding out those who are not going to be a good fit for your role.

A thorough screening process for the right candidate is time-consuming. But remember that it's also expensive to hire an employee! It costs up to 300 per cent of an employee's annual salary to replace them. You want to be sure you hire the right person, in the right seat, the first time.

But there is more than just the financial cost. There is your time—or that of the person doing the hiring—and the emotional toll it takes to hire a person. If a person makes a bad hire, they may doubt their own abilities. Why did they miss certain signs? It will also be disruptive to your team and affect their overall morale. Poor team morale could cause interpersonal conflicts between staff members, especially if they are expected to pick up the slack from a person who is unable to do the job they were hired to do.

There is also the cost associated with having a vacant role, other employees having to pick up the slack, the disrupted work environment, and potentially a negative impact on company culture.

This is why it's crucial that you make the right hire the first time. It can feel like you are pressed for time and your company cannot afford to wait and wade through a rigorous screening process. But rushing and not doing thorough background screening during the hiring process only saves you time if you're lucky. Good hiring practices are too important to leave to luck, in my opinion, and should never be rushed. Some information a background screening process can uncover can help you dodge lawsuits in the future, on top of saving you the cost and hassle of rehiring.

Putting effort into the hiring process ensures you will find suitable candidates and retain them. There is an old saying, "Hire slowly, fire quickly," which means that you shouldn't rush the hiring process but that when an employee doesn't work out, you shouldn't keep giving them more chances in the hopes that things will change for the better. During the hiring process, you should take the time and conduct the proper due diligence to ensure that you are hiring who you think you are hiring and won't need to do any firing soon.

As the first to establish ourselves in Canada's background-checking industry, in 1974, Britton Management Profiles (BMP) has been directly and indirectly setting standards and building frameworks. I, as the company's president and CEO, have found myself in a kind of ambassadorial position for the industry.

When you're the face of your industry, you must respond with razor-sharp accuracy to circumstances that couldn't have been predicted. Thankfully, I seem to be built for this kind of pressure. It's a pressure that drives me to find answers and not let myself get dragged down by fear: BMP has the potential to combust just as much as any other company. So, as each global crisis has come and gone, I've sat down with my team to devise new approaches to keep background screening contextually effective.

The roll-up-my-sleeves-and-get-it-done approach that I applied to helping my company and our industry respond and adapt after each massive event is the same approach I used to write this book. The project has been exhilarating, frightening, emotional, inspirational, thought-provoking, and exhausting at times. It's something I have been wanting to do from way before I had gathered enough language or material to write one—when I was ten.

Ten-year-old me decided on a random morning that I would write my book. It was going to be a murder mystery. I brought a TV dinner tray into my purple room, then set it up with a little stool and a pad of paper and sat down to write. I also felt that I needed to be properly dressed if I was going to do something as important as writing a book. I put on my favourite purple corduroy pants and pink top. I sat there for a while, trying to make a mystery novel come to me so that I could write it. When the story didn't magically materialize in my head as I'd expected, I quickly lost interest and went outside to play with my friends.

I was more into sports and being outside. In high school, I had a part-time job working for a clothing store in a mall. I often spent my breaks in the bookstore across the hall, and that started my love for reading. Stephen King quickly became my favourite author. He released his first novel, *Carrie*, in April 1974, and I clearly remember reading it and it becoming one of my all-time favourite books. I've read just about everything Stephen King has written ever since, including his book *On Writing: A Memoir of the Craft*.

All these decades later, I had almost forgotten that I once sat down to write a book, and that it had remained a dream for a significant chunk of my young life. It's only recently that the memory came back, with a forceful freshness, as if it had never left. In service of this old dream, I've joined a few book clubs, my favourite being a Book Accountability Group (we call ourselves the BAG ladies) run by Anne Day, who has become a mentor to me in many ways. Anne and the group helped give me the courage to write this book. I've also had the pleasure of being part of an Executive Book Club run by Laura Valvasori. We covered eight books in eight months, digging into concepts like entrepreneurial mindsets and the joys and challenges of being a business owner.

Now, finally, and coinciding with Britton Management Profiles' fiftieth anniversary, I have written the book that ten-year-old me tried to start all those years ago. It is no murder mystery, but I am also a long way from ten years old. I am writing about the one thing I am most passionate about at this point in my life. I hope this passion is apparent, and that when you are done reading, you're more confident to hire team members you can trust!

In *Screening for the One*, I share BMP's expertise to help HR professionals in making the right hire. Nothing is more crucial for someone responsible for staffing than getting to know a candidate before making an offer. Yet, because some candidates embellish, omit, and even outright lie on resumes and in interviews, you may go through the time-consuming and costly process of hiring and onboarding your newest employee, only to realize you didn't hire who you thought you were hiring—and that you need to go through the recruitment process again to find the right fit for the job.

Sometimes, clients come to us after this initial failure. I set out to write a book that assumes you haven't made the mistake yet—a preventative guide of sorts. You'll gain insights we've honed over decades of helping clients just like you reduce risk, maximize efficiency, and build stellar teams. Each chapter shares strategies for thoroughly vetting candidates.

The first section leads you through the history of BMP as well as background screening and how world events have affected the process. It dives into how the software works and why a human element is critical to the process. It also looks at why job candidates lie, and what they lie about.

The second section lays out how background screening fits into the search for the perfect job candidate, what to watch out for, and why you should utilize a screening company to keep things objective.

The third section details the different types of background screening and what each check entails, while the fourth section peels apart the importance of social media checks. This requires more in-depth understanding of the current hiring market, and I wanted to cover every aspect.

My goal is to equip you with the confidence and peace of mind that comes from truly knowing who you hire—to the furthest extent possible, at least. When you can feel good about every new addition to your team, you may start approaching your organizational goals with more confidence.

Section 1:
How We Got Here

Chapter 1:
Who Is BMP?

My father, an entrepreneur at heart, grew up watching my grandfather build a successful business, Britton's Pharmacy, in midtown Toronto. The family expected that my father would take over that business, but that wasn't his plan. On December 4, 1974, he incorporated David G. Britton & Associates, which would later become Britton Management Profiles, Inc. He had a vision and wanted to fulfil his own dreams. I was growing up while he was growing the business, and I must have soaked up some of his wisdom.

My father always had an entrepreneurial mindset. During the late 1950s and 1960s, he was employed by Retail Credit Company and was responsible for opening several offices for them across the country. He started working for them in the United States and then moved to Canada, where he managed a series of their new offices in Eastern Canada. As a result, my brother was born in St. John's, Newfoundland, and I was born in Montreal, Quebec. We spent a few of our early years in Saint John, New Brunswick before settling in Toronto, which was home to my father's family and close to my mother's family home and farm in Uxbridge, Ontario.

I loved living close to my grandparents and my tribe of cousins on the family farm in Uxbridge. My preoccupations in life were what I would wear to school the next day and what my friends and I would do after school. My world also revolved around sports. I loved playing competitive sports, especially baseball.

I wish I had had the foresight to ask my parents more questions about their lives and had been more curious. At fourteen, I had no idea what my father did for a living, only that he went to work every day. And that he worked a lot.

My mother also had an entrepreneurial mindset. She ran a marketing company from a home office where I would often do my homework. One of my first part-time jobs while I was in high school was working for her company. My job was to conduct market research interviews with people who were attending events, such as the Calgary Stampede and the Toronto Exhibition.

With David G. Britton & Associates, my father had established a path of his own outside of his family's expectations. But the pharmacy wasn't neglected—his younger brother, Grant, would soon take over. My father's first office was on Queen Street in Toronto before he moved it out to the suburbs—Don

Mills, to be specific. But he missed the downtown vibe and soon moved the office back to Toronto's Cabbagetown.

David G. Britton & Associates' primary focus in these early stages was investigative reference checking. They would receive, via courier from a client, a copy of a potential candidate's resume, and Dad's company would source out references from information provided on the resume. He would call previous employers, speak with a person who the potential candidate reported to, and ask questions related to their performance. He very quickly established a solid list of clients, and through word of mouth, the business grew.

The background-screening industry did not start to emerge, as an industry, until the 1980s. However, it was slow to gain traction, due to the recession lasting from around July 1981 to November 1982. This economic downturn was triggered by tight monetary policy put in place to fight mounting inflation. (Sound familiar?) The 1981–82 recession was the worst economic downturn in the United States and Canada since the Great Depression, at least until 2008—but I digress.

Once we emerged from that recession in 1982, the industry started to gain traction, and it was becoming common for companies to want to verify things like education credentials and employment history. The gathering of this information was still done via telephone. It was time consuming, labour intensive, and there was a significant margin for error.

We would reach out to a former employer, ask to speak with someone who was in HR, and confirm information related to a candidate's stated employment history. Response times could be lengthy.

Education verifications were often just as painful and time consuming. They were also often conducted via phone, by contacting the registrar's office of an institution and confirming information that we provided to them. Soon, the registrar's office dreaded our calls.

Employers who did criminal background checks in the 1970s and 1980s were few and far between. There wasn't as much awareness of the legal risk for employers if they hired someone with a criminal record related to a crime that had either affected someone in the workplace or involved a theft from the employer. There were, though, still criminal background checks for certain jobs back then—such as government and safety-sensitive jobs, as well as banking. They just took a long time to complete, as it was pre-internet.

In the 1990s, a growing number of employers began to recognize the need to involve professional background screening in the hiring process.

In 1994, I was working with a consulting engineering firm as a civil engineering technician—a career I thought I'd spend my life in—when my father's illness changed everything. It forced him to take a leave of absence. I was on maternity leave with my second child and had the time to step in and assist until my father recovered. Eventually, he did recover, but he was never quite the same. With the advancement of technology and the way the industry was evolving, it would have been difficult for him to manage. I then became interim president, and once we realized he would not be able to return to his previous full slate of responsibilities due to his declining health, I eventually became the permanent CEO. Over the next three decades, I became the experienced veteran of the background-screening industry my father pioneered.

Technology also started to facilitate growth of the industry, as access to data became easier. Much changed in the industry from 2000 to 2010, and going forward criminal records became routine. Privacy laws and regulations also changed. Data is now more protected. This has its advantages, but it also poses issues with obtaining the required information to make informed hiring decisions.

Then came the birth of the National Association of Professional Background Screening, or NAPBS, in 2003—an organization committed to excellence, accountability, and professionalism in the industry. The organization quickly expanded, with members from all over the world and the addition of three international councils in the years that followed. Later, it was renamed to Professional Background Screening Association, or PBSA, to reflect this globalization. It is an organization that I am actively involved in, chairing the Canadian board in 2020 and co-chairing the education board in 2024.

The PBSA provides accreditation and certifies eligible background-screening companies, mainly in the United States. When looking for an employment screening company to assist in evaluating potential employees before hiring them, I recommend opting for one with PBSA accreditation. This is the gold standard for the background-screening industry in the United States. At the time of writing, PBSA was in the process of launching a similar accreditation for background-screening companies in other countries around the world, including Canada. BMP became a global diverse supplier through

WEConnect International in 2017 and a Canadian diverse supplier with Women Business Enterprises (WBE) Canada.

In 2009, BMP started to build BORS, an online ordering system for their clients to assist in the completion of their background checks. Software for this important task was not available, so we built it from the ground up. It continues to be a work in progress, evolving as clients request new services and suppliers change. Clients have also requested customization to meet their unique requirements, and to access metrics, which has led to continued enhancements.

For example, in 2013, BMP was asked to develop an immunization tracking program for a leading pharmaceutical company. We had been conducting several pre-employment screening checks for this company, such as reference checks and education verifications, when they came to us with this particular concept. Because we had built our own screening platform, we had the ability to add this type of check to our platform. When COVID-19 hit, we added this option for all our clients. We developed the idea even further when many companies asked for immunization tracking for current employees. Immunization status is important for several industries. More about that later on.

At BMP, we continue to follow the needs of our clients and develop new and more innovative systems. This industry requires rapid adjustment to meet the needs of employers. As social networking exploded in popularity, BMP launched social media checks. We are proud of our continued dedication to innovation and our commitment to helping our clients hire the best possible candidates.

Over the decades, our custom-developed software has continually evolved as our clients' requirements and needs have changed, and it has contributed directly to our clients' success. It has also allowed us to scale in areas and ways we may not have otherwise been able to. It's given us a focal point for our innovation and creative problem-solving. In the end, it has helped us to drive growth—for us and for our clients.

Chapter 2:
How World Events
Changed Everything

Britton Management Profiles was twenty-seven years old when the first plane hit the World Trade Center in 2001. I will never forget that September morning; a perfect one as far as Toronto mornings go at that time of the year. The skies were clear blue, the air warm, with none of the summer's oppressive humidity. It was easy to feel limitless.

I drove my young children to school and then returned home to meet the electrician who was doing some work at our house. He was waiting for me in the driveway. As we entered my house, the phone was ringing—talk of great timing! It was my mother calling.

She sounded panicked as she urged me to turn on the television. I did as I was told, and all the plans I'd had for that day fizzled. The electrician and I sat for at least an hour, not speaking, just staring in horror at the replays of that first plane crashing into the World Trade Center, and then as another plane plunged into the Pentagon. The images are indelible in my mind: a magnificently blue sky smudged with smoke as the buildings tumbled to the ground.

Our world was going to change forever—that much I knew. I had no idea the magnitude of that change or how much of it my family and I were going to feel directly. Even more, I did not anticipate how much impact this one event would have on our business and how we conducted it.

What followed was fear—a sprawling kind with icy fingers that reached inside each of us and gripped whole nations at the same time. There was much to be fearful about: the loss of life, scale of destruction, our vulnerability, uncertainty, and later, the economic consequences. Because the general climate was filled with fear, it was unsurprising when companies started approaching the hiring process with unprecedented caution. It was clear that these were fragile times, and that the target as well as the culprit in horrific acts like 9/11, could be anyone. It was a cautiousness that bordered on paranoia, but justifiably so.

I had been leading BMP for seven years, just as my father had for twenty years before that, on the day those crashing planes changed our world. We had entered the industry as the first reference-checking/background-screening firm in Canada. Being the first meant BMP assessed the hiring scene and, without having a pre-existing template to work with, created the solutions that were an exact answer to the problem employers were facing when trying to verify applicant references and other credentials. Over the next two-and-a-half decades, we have fine-tuned that original formula that worked for us and continues to work for us and our clients. It has been a continuous learning process and an effort to solve problems for our clients.

So, when 9/11 and the collective fear that came with it hit, it dented everything, including our clients' and potential clients' focus on what was necessary in a background check. We lost trust in who we were bringing into our companies. For the first time, most employers wanted—needed—to know a potential candidate's criminal history before hiring them. Before 9/11, criminal record checks were only needed for certain types of roles; the more sensitive the role, the higher the likelihood an employer would want to be certain of a candidate's trustworthiness which, in part, was determined through their criminal records report. But now, most of our clients want to know about *any* candidate's criminal history, for *any* role. We have risen to that occasion and have continued to adjust with each major event we have lived through, including the 2008 recession, and more recently, the COVID-19 pandemic.

Among the many things COVID-19 brought with it is the need for identity verification and immunization tracking. If a company wanted to stay in business or continue operations, in most cases that meant embracing remote work arrangements for their employees. If they had to hire someone, also remotely, how did they know who they were really hiring? It was during this time that BMP launched an identity verification tool to ensure the person you were interviewing via video call was really who they said they were.

As John F. Kennedy once said, "We would like to live as we once lived, but history will not permit it." World events have continued to shape and change what we do. What is critical is that we adapt and adjust to ensure we do great work and know who we are bringing into our companies.

I have loved watching the pre-employment screening industry develop over the years. Every year at our annual PBSA conference, I'm privileged to meet with background-screening companies from around the world. I've met international partners at these conferences who later became key partners that helped us with the verification of things like foreign educational qualifications. I'm also able to gain valuable insights on what is happening in the industry and future trends to be aware of, such as the impact of artificial intelligence (AI) or retina scanning.

Society and technology are always changing, and it pays to pay attention to how these changes affect the background-screening industry or require us to change and adapt.

Chapter 3:
The Truth Is,
Job Candidates Lie

When I was fourteen, I had only one career ambition. I wanted to work at a certain well-known fast-food restaurant chain. I envisioned myself as that happy employee who greeted their customers and asked to take their orders. One day I walked into my local fast-food restaurant like I owned the place and asked to speak to the manager. I told him I wanted to work there. He asked me how old I was, and—I lied.

"Fifteen," I said. After all, I would *soon* be fifteen. In just a few months. And guess what? I got the job. I was so excited; I told all my friends to come in on my first day and I would serve them. On that first day, I was shocked when they sent me down into a dark dingy classroom in the basement with a bunch of other new employees to be taught about customer service. I was nowhere near where I could serve my friends. But I did learn critical life skills that I still use today.

Back then, I was naïve. Today, my adult background-screening-professional self is horrified that I was one of those candidates who lie during the job application process. However innocent my teenage scenario may seem, it is part of a much larger problem: A staggering thirty per cent of job seekers have lied or bent the truth on their resumes. That means that whenever reviewing a resume, there is nearly a one in three chance you're looking at information that has been embellished in some way or doesn't paint the complete picture.

There are job candidates who will stretch the truth as far as the North Pole. In my experience, the extent of embellishment can be shocking.

Why Do They Lie?

Wouldn't it be great if we lived in a world where people were always honest? Imagine it: All cover letters from job candidates would be chock-full of great things that they really did. Then you'd move on to an equally truthful resume. And, when you're sitting across the table from them during an interview, it'd be a guarantee that you could take their word on whatever it is they said.

A candidate would tell you, out of the goodness of their heart, that the explanation for that five-year gap in their resume was that they served time in prison for fraud. You'd think, "Oh, good thing you mentioned that just before I hired you because this role involves handling sensitive information," so you'd move on, not having wasted your time. Another candidate would tell you that even though the job specifically requires more than five years of experience, they only have two, and their references aren't quite as strong as they need to be. Yet they happen to have the biggest passion for this specific role, they have thoroughly researched your company and want to work for you, they learn quickly while on the job, and they have a good attitude. Now you must weigh whether you're willing to take a chance on someone who has the right soft skills and the potential to grow into the technical requirements, against the risks of hiring an underqualified candidate for a high-stakes role. How much easier it would be to hire!

Honesty and integrity are highly valued qualities in the workplace. While most candidates are honest and ethical, a large percentage of candidates do misrepresent themselves.

There are many reasons why people lie. When a potential candidate sends you their information, hoping to land a role that could change their life, the need to win the job can easily outweigh the risks of being caught in a lie. The stakes are high and impressing you—the potential employer—is paramount. It can be hard for a job seeker to look competitive on paper, even for roles for which they are qualified. Like all competitions, some succumb to the pressure to go to great lengths to enhance their chances of winning, just like athletes caught up in doping scandals.

So, when a person is desperate to get a job, especially that dream job that they have been working towards for years, they may be more inclined to lie. Sometimes, it is not so much lying as omitting important details to slightly misrepresent their employment history or education. But a lie is still a lie.

A potential candidate may lie in hopes it will help them secure a better offer when it comes time to negotiate compensation, or out of fear of discrimination based on their age, gender, race, or other factors. They may lie to cover up a gap in their employment history that is due to something they fear will be negatively perceived, like serving prison time.

The main reason, however, is it's a method that works. And it works because most of the time, the potential employer is not checking. Hiring managers end up enabling this fraudulent behaviour through lax hiring processes.

What Do They Lie About?

If it *can* be lied about, some candidates *are* lying about it. I have seen candidates lie about their qualifications, their experience, their education, their current or previous salary. Employment and education verifications are what a job candidate will lie about the most. It may not be an outright, totally fabricated lie but something simple and seemingly innocuous.

Employment History

Many people have gaps in their employment history. Maybe they were dealing with an illness, or maybe they were taking time off to travel, or they were in prison, or they were raising kids or taking care of an elderly parent. Or maybe they lost their previous job unexpectedly and struggled to find a new one. When coming to the competitive job-seeking playing field, this can feel like just another thing that's working against them.

A potential job candidate may even invent a company on their resume, appoint themselves president or business owner, and claim that this is where they "worked" during the gap years. Jobs reported as self-employment can be a flag to trigger further investigation. In our experience at BMP, we've seen that some of the most relevant details for assessing a candidate's suitability for a role can be hidden behind these ghost companies.

Candidates may also lie about other aspects of their employment history. For example, they sometimes give false start and end dates for working in a certain job, to meet the minimum years of experience required. They may also misrepresent their role, job duties, and salary. And they often lie about their reason for leaving that job. After all, who would want to employ someone who was fired from a previous job for stealing or for sexual harassment?

Education

The spectrum of misrepresentation of educational qualifications spans from those who started but did not finish their degree programs from real universities to those claiming to have attended institutions that do not exist, all the way to the other end of the scale, of presenting false certifications from diploma mills.

Diploma mills, which are businesses that sell illegitimate diplomas or academic degrees for a fee, are becoming more common, enabling potential candidates to misrepresent their education. Recently, we had a candidate claim she had completed her Personal Support Worker—or PSW—diploma program. She sent us documentation from the National Association of Career Colleges—or the NACC—to prove it. When we sent the documentation to the NACC to verify its authenticity, we learned it was fake and the person had never attended. We discovered that this person had been working as a PSW illegally for years, potentially endangering the health and welfare of those in her care.

Typically, we find that if a candidate does not include words like *degree*, *diploma*, or *certificate* in their credentials, or indicate that specifically on their resume or LinkedIn profile, it likely means they did not graduate and do not have the qualification they studied for. "Bachelor of Arts, University of Toronto 2017–2020" is not necessarily the same as "Bachelor of Arts Degree, University of Toronto 2017–2020."

There may or may not be a more complex truth behind the omission of that one word. Are they misrepresenting the truth by leaving out the word *degree*? This can be your cue to dig a little deeper to find out if this was an honest omission, an attempt to skirt an important detail, or a truthful representation of an educational program they participated in but did not complete. You know the requirements for the position, so this one little flag is your cue to check further to make sure you're vetting candidates with the qualifications you need.

References

We've also seen candidates list friends instead of valid professional references. When our associate conducts the reference interview and is unable to get information from the reference on what, specifically, the candidate did, their reason for leaving, or any other relevant information, it quickly becomes clear this is not a business-related reference. It is easy to spot a planted reference.

Criminal Record History

Many employers are put off when a candidate has a criminal record, especially if they've done some jail time. This is especially true when the nature of the crime is incompatible with the type of job the person is applying for. Anybody would be reluctant to employ a former bank robber as a security guard, for instance, or let someone who has been to prison for crimes involving minors work in a school. Employers may even be held liable if they hire someone with a criminal past who then goes on to harm someone in or through their workplace.

This makes it extremely difficult for candidates who have a criminal past, but who have been fully rehabilitated, to find employment. And so, they may feel compelled to lie about their criminal record.

Identification

Sometimes, candidates really aren't who they say they are. Literally. Sometimes, they use a stolen identity to get the job, for example, when their immigration status precludes them from working in the country.

But the rise of remote recruiting, onboarding, and employment, combined with advances in technology, has meant a marked increase in deepfakes, where the person is completely fabricated.

Chapter 4:
The Human Element

The use of technology makes pre-employment screening easier, more efficient, and more secure. But there is no replacing the human element in the background-screening process—and at BMP, human analytics is critical. But before I dive into those human analytics, let's talk about technology.

In 1974, when clients needed our investigative reference-checking services, they would send a physical copy of a potential candidate's resume to our downtown Toronto office via courier. Usually, time was of the essence, and since the internet did not yet exist, Canada Post or courier were the usual methods. There's little that's paper based in the process today.

It was soon into my time at BMP, in 1994, that I felt the need to improve and automate processes within the company. We started requiring documents by fax rather than courier, for example, and expanding our service offerings. We started to see a need to check against fraud and to verify education credentials.

The Great Recession of 2008–09 was a tipping point for BMP. I'd already lived through one recession, in the 1980s, and it was at its worst right as I was supposed to be graduating. At that time, I took the opportunity to stay in school a little longer, upgrading my civil engineer technician designation to technologist, and I also added a project management certificate. No point hitting the job market when no one was hiring! I took the same lesson to heart during the 2008–09 recession, and BMP took advantage of the business slowdown. We improved our internal processes and built productivity tools so that we were positioned to come out stronger on the other side of that recession. And we did.

Online Requisition

During that recession, we started designing what would become our first online order system for our clients. It was a long, worthwhile process. BMP launched BORS, the Britton Online Requisition System, in 2012. It allows our clients to order their requests online, to view results 24/7, and to be notified of the completion of individual checks as we proceed with the work on their file. With BORS, a client can order the type of check they want, such as references, education, employment, criminal, credit, or social media. It also provides a wide range of metrics for our clients, like the number of checks ordered and a breakdown of the type of products ordered.

Why didn't we—and why don't we—simply purchase or license pre-employment-screening software ready-built by someone else? The challenge for the BMP team is that there are limited options for third-party pre-employment software that can be used in Canada. The United States has been quicker to develop these systems: In fact, US-based screening platforms are big business today. At BMP, we aren't comfortable using a US-centric pre-employment software. It's important that any software we use complies with Canadian laws and regulations, both national and provincial, including the *Personal Information Protection and Electronic Documents Act* (PIPEDA). It's also important that our data and all personal candidate information is stored on servers located in Canada. It's why BMP still, for the most part, builds our own custom platforms that allow clients to place orders, make requests, view results, and retrieve reports.

Once all aspects of the request are completed, a member of the BMP team is required to review the results and rate each of the individual checks we've completed using a traffic-light system.

- Green means that the report is clear and good to go.
- Yellow is a caution, and it means the client should slow down and have a look at the report before making a final decision. A yellow caution flag could mean, for example, that we confirmed that a candidate was employed by a company as indicated on their documentation, but that the dates of employment or perhaps the position do not match with what the candidate provided.

- Red indicates our client should stop and seriously take time to view the results. There is something that absolutely requires their attention—for instance, there's no record at all of the candidate having ever been employed at the company they say they've worked for. Because our clients are often pressed for time, we don't want them to miss important parts of the report.

Once a report is finalized, our clients are notified electronically. They are required to log in to our secure site and retrieve the results, as the BMP team does not send copies of a final report via email, for security reasons.

Human Analytics

We can't live without automation, but neither can we do our pre-employment background screening without a heavy dose of the human element. Human analytics means taking the time to ensure not just that a job is done properly, but that the client understands what the results are telling them.

Human analytics is the examination and processing of information that requires interpretation by a human to draw a conclusion. This is an important part of what is required when conducting a background check. When the BMP team completes a background-check report for our clients, we take the time to review each individual check. We then rate each check individually, as well as rating the overall report.

Human analytics has been an important part of our process since day one. In fact, in the early years of our existence, human analytics was all that was available to us. But this is a very important part of what we do at BMP. Every report completed by the BMP team must undergo a human analytics component before it is finalized. The reason we've always done this is to assist each client with a quick overview of their report. Clients need information quickly. They may have multiple candidates who have applied for a position within their company, and they simply don't have the time to pore over the details of each of our completed reports. Depending on the position they're hiring for, they may have ordered a variety of checks. The quality control of that final human element allows for an overview of the finer details.

Human analytics is a critical component of our reference-check process. There is a real art to the reference interviewing process. If conducted properly, a professional reference is a good indicator of how a candidate will perform for you. Each BMP team member has a cognitive advantage over any machine—yes, even in these early days of AI. They're not only evaluating the raw data. If a transcript of their conversation was to be created, it would still not reveal all the elements they're accessing to apply their judgement to that final report. We conduct references via phone and not email. And we ensure the same BMP associate completes all reference checks for one candidate and evaluates the results. It's not just about what the reference is saying, but also what they aren't. What pauses, hesitations, and stammers are there?

The BMP team starts by sending an email to the referee to ask when a good time is to have an actual conversation. We will not send a list of questions via email, because there's no way to know the referee has not sent the list of questions to the candidate who is applying for the job, to assist in answering them. It's also important to verify the credentials of the person you are speaking with when conducting a business reference. We recommend validating the reference on LinkedIn and any other source you might have access to, to confirm they are who they say they are.

Another area where human analytics are indispensable is in our social media check processes. Although we do use technology to gather all the social media content and data related to an individual candidate, that information is always reviewed and rated by a human. If our client does not have time to read a detailed report, they can have confidence in the background-checking results for their potential candidate.

Applying human analytics adds a layer of interpretation onto all the tech we use during our processes. Having a human make a conclusion rather than leaving it up to a machine, while letting technology do the early parts of the job that a human may have taken too long to do or not done nearly as well, helps create confidence in our results, even during the busiest hiring seasons.

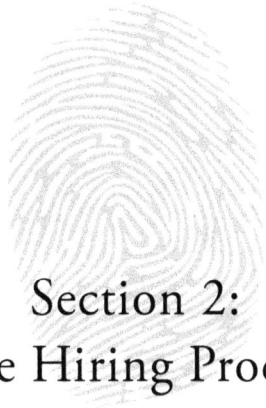

Section 2:
The Hiring Process

Chapter 5:
Starting the Search
For the Right Hire

Imagine you have a team member called Mark, who works in the sales department. No one can hit sales targets like he can! If you're looking at the numbers, and only those numbers, you're probably ready to give him a raise. Or a promotion. Or both.

But there is a problem. Mark is a pain to work with. He knows he's the best at hitting his targets and he likes to remind everyone of that fact. Just last week, he said to Jane, "It's too bad you're never going to hit my targets. You're just not cutting it." But you know Jane thrives best with encouragement. Different personalities are fuelled differently, and your team members aren't just people who work for your company but people who belong to families: people with friends, goals, likes, dislikes, and maybe most of all, boundaries. When, after months of an onslaught of snide remarks from one of your company's top performers, seven workers in total quit, the impact reverberates through the company. The most obvious effect of this is on total sales. Now that seven people are gone, Mark's contributions alone are miniscule. The company will now go through a period of loss until you can put together a new team. His behaviour has cost you money, and lots of it—despite his great individual performance. So how did it happen that Mark got hired in the first place?

Well, it's a common scenario, unfortunately. If a replacement for a position can't be filled quickly, there is the real risk the company won't move forward at all. Emergencies arise. Pressure can drive those leading an organization or those hiring to rush through a recruitment process and hire the first person who meets the technical criteria. It's an innocent kind of hiring haste, but damaging, nevertheless. Reference checks, if done properly, are a goldmine for detecting cultural fit, attitude, and behavioural red flags, but are often rushed or not completed at all. Hello, Mark.

If you do need to let go of someone from the team because you gave in to the pressure and hired too quickly, then you shouldn't hesitate in letting them go, because the cost of waiting too long can be huge. Remember: Hire slowly; fire quickly. Yes, this is easier said than done.

Unless you are in the almost non-existent segment of the population that enjoys firing people, it makes sense to aim to get your hiring process so perfect that there will be no need to fire a team member who just doesn't fit, and even less risk that you'll lose other good employees because you hired and then hesitated to fire a bad one.

You'll benefit from being calm and strategic far more than hiring fast in full panic mode. Listen to your gut during the interviews and the reference checks and ensure that those managing your pre-employment screening are doing the same. This is where you need to know that behind the curtains, a background-screening company that has never met your candidate, and therefore has no pre-existing biases, is obtaining and verifying all the appropriate information and conducting reference checks objectively. You want all the certainty you can get, and so even if it feels like the company will crumble if you don't hire by next week, prioritizing the proper due diligence is never the wrong move. At BMP, we take the emotion out of the process. We remain objective and work closely with HR teams to ensure they hire the best candidate for the job.

Even when you do take the time and get your hiring process right, you still need to go through onboarding and training, and it can be a significant amount of time before the new hire can be productive. During this period, your team is straining under the added responsibilities, which can easily develop into a crisis, depending on the nature of additional roles each has to take. So, you want to hire and *keep* your hires because you want to reduce employee burnout, decrease hiring costs, maximize productivity, and encourage team morale. Additionally, you want to promote company growth and save time and money. An employee with a genuine, verified track record of excellence is great for the team, as they will likely introduce new ideas and perspectives on top of doing their regular job well.

So, to reiterate: if you do your homework well during the hiring process, you reduce the odds of ever needing to fire anyone.

Your Hiring Ecosystem

Your homework for your hiring process begins well before you start evaluating candidates or doing background checks. Before you start actively recruiting candidates, it helps to be clear on what the job entails and the kind of person you'd ideally like to do that job. This way, you can streamline the process, and you'll know what to focus on once the recruitment process has started. It will also help you decide which background checks you'll need.

Here's a list of documents you'll want to create before you start recruiting, so you can iron out the details and be clear on exactly what you want in the candidate who will fulfil this role.

Ideal Candidate Profile

The ideal candidate profile is an internal document and is the most important one, since it gives everyone involved in the hiring process a clear idea of what you are looking for, and you can focus every step of the recruitment process towards finding that person.

As the name suggests, the ideal candidate profile describes in detail the ideal person for the role. Naturally, you want them to have a specific set of skills and experience. However, you also need to look at what their preferences are—their most productive work style, as it were—as well as what lights them on fire. This helps reveal how your company and the role might appeal to them.

What you are looking for in the ideal candidate depends on the position they're applying for, as well as factors like your company culture. Here is an example of a profile for the ideal candidate for the role of brand activation manager in a growing eco-friendly cosmetics company.

Ideal Candidate Profile Example

Brand Activation Manager: The Ideal Candidate
Their strengths:
- Writing, editing of a variety of content
- Flair for marketing and online engagement and understands a variety of social platforms, how audiences use them, and how to best position the brand to leverage each one
- Ability to see the big picture and connect many moving parts to work towards the big picture
- Ability to see, mimic, or recommend and then create content in our brand voice so that it resonates with intended audience
- Understands audience profiling, demographic, psychographic, and geographic factors, their needs and wants, to identify opportunities in brand content gaps
- Ability to connect content requirements with situational, client, and brand needs, and able to either find existing content or create it

- Self-governed, self-motivated, and the ability to work alone while also being a good team member
- Organized and able to follow procedures and policies (e.g. naming conventions) while also able to recommend improvements they see
- Ability to multitask, meet tight deadlines, and perform under pressure
- Solution and client oriented
- Ability to learn and apply the learnings to specific situations
- Conflict resolution and problem solving and the ability to stay calm when others are not
- Thrives on helping others
- Decisive and action oriented
- Embraces technology and systems to ensure success of personal, brand, and team goals
- Priority management and the ability to work in the day-to-day granular details while striving to meet strategic objectives
- Thorough and accurate
- Ability to positively represent the brand
- Punctual and reliable
- Diplomatic, with strong leadership skills
- Confidence to praise in public and provide constructive criticism in private
- Ability to work in situations that may be ambiguous (e.g. a need may arise that was not foreseen at the point of hiring, and it becomes part of their role moving forward)

Their weaknesses:
- May generate more content at a faster pace than manager can keep up with from a review/approval perspective
- May recommend implementation of processes, approaches, or content strategies the company is not quite ready for
- May overstep and provide recommendations where they're not needed

Their core values:
- High integrity
- Values genuine relationships
- Self-awareness and reflection for personal growth
- Passion for creative expression

Their key skill sets:
- Experience working with diverse, long-form and short-form content created for a variety of purposes and to make judgements about what is required with each
- Content planning, strategic thinking
- Organization skills
- Ability to see and set growth targets, e.g. social footprint, engagements, followers, and understanding how to work towards growing in a way that is meaningful to brand revenue
- Understanding of and experience with content platforms, needs, concepts

- Effective communication and problem solving
- Use of technology for process efficiency
- Listening

Key things they are looking for in a job:
- What excites them?
  - Being able to work from home/freedom/flexibility
  - Being able to contribute in a meaningful way to a growing company
  - Opportunities for advancement as the brand grows
  - Ability to contribute to helping grow brand visibility and engagement
  - Alignment with our brand's core values
- How do they want to feel about their work?
  - Engaged
  - In the inner circle/in the know/included
  - Committed
  - Adding significant and unique value
  - Rewarded
- What are their goals?
  - Work for a brand where they have lots of potential for contribution and growth
  - Grow within a company long term
  - A significant leadership role in a cool brand
  - Skill development
  - Opportunity to be promoted
  - Career advancement

- What could they be fearful of?
  - Not doing as much of what they love
  - Challenges with time zone differences
  - Being tracked by technology
  - Lack of security
  - Lack of benefits
  - Lack of structure for their job description, as the role requires someone able to be fluid
  - Fear of the unknown
  - Leaving friends behind

Preferences and abilities (core competencies/behaviours)
1. Advanced writing/editing and content creation skills
2. Understanding of content dissemination practices, how the platforms work
3. Strives for excellence
4. Embraces adding value to audiences
5. Enjoys multitasking and revels in competing deadlines (prioritize/judgement strength)
6. Loves helping others achieve their goals
7. Tenacious
8. Self-directed, motivated, and composed
9. Leadership
10. Judgement to know when to reach out for support and approval and when it is safe and appropriate to proceed without it

Opportunity Profile

The opportunity profile is a document created with your ideal candidate in mind, to be shared externally with those candidates who seem to meet the initial screening criteria for your role. It's designed to help them self-identify further once they've been enticed by your job ad—in fact, it is a longer version of your job ad.

Here's an example of an opportunity profile for a content marketing role in an eco-friendly cosmetics company.

Opportunity Profile Example

Are you an excellent communicator and marketing specialist with a passion for writing and editing a variety of content, from letters to web content to ad copy? Do you have a passion for the eco-friendly cosmetics industry, and for work that helps change the lives of others for the better? Are you already plugged into and aware of current events and influencers in the eco-friendly cosmetics space?

Do you love the freedom and flexibility of being an independent contractor working from home, or wherever you may be in the world? Are you always online and connected?

Do you plan marketing content calendars in your sleep, seeing how cross-platform content dripping campaigns help build brand awareness and audience engagement?

Are you looking for an opportunity to grow through a long-term relationship with an inspiring and passionate company that sets out to make the world a better place? Do you operate based on a clear set of core values and prefer working for brands that do the same?

If this sounds like you, consider joining EcoSkin Cosmetics as content marketer. In this role, you will:

- Create and activate our content strategy and planning calendar
- Create/edit/review content that supports brand goals, including but not limited to podcast intros, blogs, articles, social media captions/content, email content, newsletters, advertising copy
- Keep projects up to date in our project management and tracking system
- Work within a virtual team environment
- Maintain current material on websites and our other relevant apps and platforms
- Monitor and keep social media profiles up to date, lead engagement efforts on our social platforms including our website
- Manage email marketing lists, communications, webforms, embed codes, lead magnets, email marketing system integration with website
- Prepare and present monthly reports on progress towards brand goals

Characteristics of ideal candidate
- Self-starter who takes initiative
- Respectful, diplomatic, flexible, courageous, dedicated, loyal, adaptable, ethical
- Organized and efficient

Desired experience
- Experience in cosmetics industry
- Knowledge of and experience with Wordpress, SEO, Google Analytics

- Comfortable with Google Drive, Word, Excel, project management systems
- Experience managing Facebook groups and as an admin of other profiles

Compensation:
Monthly budget to be discussed during exploration with suitable candidates.

Job Ad

Your job ad is crafted from your opportunity profile and is, of course, what you post externally, via job boards and apps. It can also be sent directly to interested parties that meet your initial screening criteria.

Here's an example, based on the same marketing role used in the previous examples.

Job Ad Example: Marketing and Publicity

Are you a marketing and publicity expert with a passion for helping companies showcase their products/services and find clients? Do you love helping brands achieve sales, revenue, and visibility targets, and do you love doing work that helps change the lives of others for the better?

Do you whip up marketing strategies before lunchtime, instinctively seeing beyond traditional marketing activities to industry, stakeholder, and collaborator opportunities?

Are you looking for an opportunity to work with an inspiring and passionate company that sets out to make the world a better place? Do you operate based on a clear set of core values and prefer working for brands that do the same?

If this sounds like you, consider applying for this marketing and publicity role at EcoSkin Cosmetics.

Responsibilities and Deliverables
In this role, you will:

- Lead marketing efforts for select product/service lines
- Prepare marketing plans for executive review and approval, and implement them
- Write, distribute, and custom-pitch media releases, story pitches, or interview opportunities
- Coordinate events, as needed
- Plan and coordinate social media content and ad campaigns
- Ensure brand is appropriately referenced and visible in all author/book marketing materials and activities
- Uphold company's core values, brand standards, and client experience practices
- Regularly report on campaign progress and achievements

Desired Experience

- Extensive marketing and publicity experience working in the industry
- Media relations and strategic communications background
- Industry-relevant media contacts a bonus

If this sounds like you, please complete and submit this questionnaire before October 31, 12 p.m. EST. [Don't forget to add the time zone, especially when you're hiring people who will be working remotely!]

About Us

EcoSkin Cosmetics is a young cosmetics company that wants people to look their best while helping to make the world a better place. We create skincare, hair care, and personal hygiene products that are eco-friendly, using only sustainably produced and responsibly obtained ingredients. [Keep this description of who you are and what you do short and to the point—two sentences.]

Pre-screening Questions

Include pre-screening questions in your application process to gather additional contextual information about candidates. Once the applications start pouring in, you can send a brief list of pre-screening questions to candidates who seem qualified and ask them to submit written responses. This is another layer of information to help you create a shortlist of candidates to invite to your interview process.

Pre-screening questions help you determine whether the applicant has done their homework or whether they're simply bulk applying for anything and everything, regardless of suitability.

Example questions for your pre-screening questionnaire include:

1. What's one surprising thing you've discovered about our company?
2. Describe the character strengths you would bring to this role.
3. Describe your professional/experiential strengths that make you a good fit for this role.
4. What motivates you?
5. What interpersonal skills do you have? Do you prefer to work on your own, or do you like being part of a team?
6. Tell us what excites you about this role, and why you're interested in it.
7. Tell us what scares you about this role.
8. If you were to take an additional course, what would you sign up for?
9. Which areas for development/improvement can you identify?
10. Please review the content on our website and then describe who you think our target audience/ideal customer/ideal client is.
11. Please outline your rates, fees, or expectations around compensation.

Interview Guide

Having an interview guide ready before you start the interviewing process will help you decide which questions to ask and what to look for to get the most complete picture of the candidate during the interview.

You'll base your interview guide off your opportunity profile and job description, crafting a mix of questions that help you see beyond the qualifications and experience the candidate has listed on their resume. Include "Tell us about a time when" questions that will prompt the candidate to share their approaches to problem solving, navigating challenging circumstances, how well they think on their feet, and decision making.

Try to ask as many open-ended questions as possible, since this encourages conversation.

Offer Letter

Your offer letter can be an upbeat, welcome-aboard letter that helps inspire your lead candidate to accept your offer and helps them see the potential for them in the role. Incorporate language from your opportunity profile and emphasize their contribution to the company's goals and objectives. Include what a typical day would look like.

If there are any special requirements for the job, such as travel or having to work on weekends, let the candidate know upfront, since this may be an issue for some, especially those candidates who are caring for children or other family members.

Your offer letter should also include start date and have all compensation information clearly laid out, including vacation time and benefits, but save all the legalese for the employment agreement.

Employment Agreement

Your employment agreement is where you provide even more detail about expectations in the role, compensation, and the conditions under which you would terminate. (This is where you cover your a$$, also known as CYA).

With all this information prepared—before you even begin to advertise your vacant position—you are now ready to proceed with your recruitment.

Chapter 6:
Finding the Right Candidate

Once you've posted your job ads and started the recruitment process, the applications will start pouring in. One of these candidates will be perfect for the job; the challenge now is to find them.

Wading Through the Sea of Candidates

Dealing with many job applicants can be time consuming and overwhelming, but there are different strategies you can use to effectively move through the pool of candidates and identify the most suitable ones for closer screening and potential interviews.

Use Automated Screening Tools

Today, there are many applicant tracking systems (ATS) on the market, allowing you to filter candidates based on specific keywords, qualifications, and experience. This can significantly reduce the time spent reviewing applications manually. These systems can be costly, so make sure the system you choose will give you exactly what you need. You don't want to pay for a robust and expensive system and only use a small portion of its offerings.

Prioritize Key Qualifications

Identify the must-have qualifications and skills for the role. As you review applications, prioritize candidates who meet these essential criteria.

If you find that there aren't many applicants who meet the requirements and you'd like to keep your options open, you can always create a B group of candidates that may fall short on one or two criteria, but where it's possible to work around that.

Group Review

Consider involving a small team of relevant stakeholders to review applications. Each member can focus on specific aspects, such as qualifications, experience, cultural fit, or behavioural characteristics, and then share their insights for a more comprehensive evaluation.

Set Time Limits

Allocate a specific amount of time to review each application. This prevents spending too much time on individual applications and ensures a more efficient process.

Create a Scoring System

Develop a scoring system to objectively evaluate candidates based on key criteria. This can help you compare and rank candidates more effectively.

Continuous Feedback and Improvement

As you proceed through the hiring process, gather feedback from your team and evaluate the effectiveness of your screening methods. Adjust as needed to streamline the process. Feedback may assist in keeping you ahead of your competitors by having a mindset for improvement.

Interviews and Reference Checks

I know it isn't always possible in today's geographically diverse work environment, but if you have an option to hold your interviews face-to-face, it is always better. Via video call is the second-best option, followed by telephone and then written question and answers.

If you choose to conduct interviews with a select group of candidates who have passed through some initial screenings, use a structured interview process with standardized questions. This allows for fairer and more consistent evaluations across all candidates.

It's also important to ensure you can ask open-ended questions in this process. An open-ended question cannot be answered with a one-word yes or no answer. A great strategy is to start questions with "Tell me about a time when…" These questions require a candidate to think about their response and draw upon a real-life example. This will give you far more insight than you can find by reading their resume.

Also ensure you ask about their areas of development. If they could sign up for any course, what would they sign up for?

Video Interviews

Conducting initial video interviews can provide more insight into a candidate's communication skills, professionalism, and demeanor and help narrow down the pool before inviting candidates for in-person interviews. For example, if they didn't make any effort to look presentable but instead are clearly wearing their pajamas, it could be a red flag about how seriously they will take the job, especially when working from home.

Reference Checks

Once you've identified your top candidates, don't give in to the temptation to treat reference checks as optional or a mere formality. You're verifying their skills, experience, and work history.

Chapter 10 discusses reference checks more in depth, but we strongly encourage you to conduct reference checks via telephone. The BMP team has had concerns with sending references via email. How do you know who is answering the questions?

Even better is to outsource reference checks to a professional reference-checking firm. They remain objective: Having not met the candidate, they have no preconceived ideas. Also, a third party has no pressure to fill the position and can maintain distance. They know when to listen to the hesitations and probe deeply when the referee is not forthcoming with information.

Keep Communication Transparent

Keep candidates informed about the progress of their application. Transparency can help maintain a positive candidate experience, even for those who are not selected. It also assists in building trust and positive word of mouth.

It's important that your company maintains a good reputation. People don't want to work for a company that has a bad reputation.

Evaluating the Whole Candidate

When your job is to identify the candidate most likely to succeed in a role and then set them up as best as you can, it's important that you know exactly what needs to be at the top of your mind. In other words, how do you know them when you see them? What basics are you ticking off your list?

Culture Fit

You're hiring into an existing company culture. Assess that culture—or even better, create it—then hire soulmates for your organization. Company culture encompasses the collective values, beliefs, behaviour, and work style of the employees.

Finding those candidates who align well with your company culture is critical for the success of your business. Employees who identify more with their employer tend to be happier, more satisfied with their jobs, and more committed to the organization, and they tend to experience greater job satisfaction. They integrate more easily into existing teams, contribute positively to the work atmosphere, and are more likely to stay with the company.

Qualifications

This is where many of your candidates are most likely to misrepresent themselves. Professional qualifications encompass a candidate's education, skills, certifications, designations, and relevant background. These factors are essential in determining whether the candidate has the necessary knowledge as well as the expertise to perform the job effectively. They help provide a potential employer with an idea of what a candidate is equipped to accomplish. The better the credentials they have, the greater the likelihood that they can deliver the output you will require of them.

Pay close attention in this area. Ensuring that a candidate meets the minimum qualifications for a role is crucial to ensure they can handle the job responsibilities competently.

Experience

Experience is the depth and relevance of the candidate's past work history and achievements. Relevant experience can indicate a candidate's ability to handle the specific tasks and challenges associated with the role.

But you must look at experience in terms of both its relevance and its depth. How advanced is the candidate in their career path? Experience provides candidates with opportunities to learn from successes and failures.

It's also critical to verify the information that they are providing to you about their work experience. This can be done easily if you are conducting quality reference checks where you ask the referee about the tasks the candidate performed for them, whether these were part of the job description or not.

Behavioural Characteristics

At times, a candidate with less experience but the right skillset and attitude can be a valuable addition to any team. Behavioural characteristics can provide clues as to how well a candidate will interact with colleagues, handle conflicts, and contribute to a positive work environment. These characteristics include a potential candidate's personality traits, communication style, problem-solving abilities, teamwork skills, as well as emotional intelligence. Emotional intelligence is the ability to identify and regulate a person's emotions, as well as understand the emotions of others.

Scientific assessments such as reliable and reputable personality tests can give you a glimpse into a candidate's behavioural attributes. We recommend our clients use these behavioural assessments or personality test tools to help them observe, describe, explain, and predict a candidate's behaviour and better understand how candidates might fit into your team and company culture. Be aware though that there are various factors that can affect the outcome of a personality test, including the candidate being able to fake their answers.

Finding the Right Balance

What if a candidate has a great personality that happens to fit almost perfectly with your company culture, but is a little lacking on the qualifications and experience front? What takes precedence in your decision-making?

The answer is that the approach to evaluating the whole candidate's suitability for the role isn't linear. Overall, you want to aim for balance between culture fit, behavioural traits, qualifications, and experience—and you won't find the key to assessing this balance buried in the technology. It takes human analytics and judgement. What the right balance is will depend on your company, the scope of the job, and how much room you can give them to learn as they go.

I've seen the magnetic pull that leads many hiring managers to put experience and qualifications on a pedestal. There are two main problems with this:

1. As soon as a candidate checks the boxes on these two, concessions are made, or signs are ignored in terms of

how well their personality will fit into the organization's culture. The problem with this approach is that you can get highly qualified candidates who do not get along with the team, whose values clash with the values of the brand, who bring down the productivity of those around them through their behaviour, and who ultimately can't stay in the organization long term—either they leave, or they need to be fired.

2. Overqualified people can quickly become bored in a role because it does not challenge them to their full capacity. And underqualified candidates can easily get overwhelmed by the pace of things.

Incorporating a comprehensive approach that considers each of these factors separately and then together will help you find the right job candidate who not only meets the technical requirements of the job, but also contributes to the overall health of your organization, team dynamics, productivity, and long-term success.

Patience

Keep in mind that it will likely take time to find the right candidate. Patience is a virtue and a must, especially in a challenging job market. You need to both efficiently review applications and ensure thorough evaluation of each candidate. And using a combination of automated tools and predefined criteria can help you be successful in navigating through hundreds of candidates to find the best one. The entire pre-employment screening process can take from a few hours to days, depending on the types of checks that you require. When international checks are required, it can even take a few weeks. By using all the tools to your advantage, you can streamline this process.

On top of hard facts, we also recommend to our clients that they listen to their gut feeling about a person, always, throughout the entire recruitment process. This is a skill that can be strengthened when you learn to trust your intuition. If something does not seem right, it's generally not!

Chapter 7:
Should You Do
Your Own Screening?

Many HR teams know the importance of conducting a wide range of pre-employment screening checks when onboarding a new employee. The debate is not usually whether one should be done or not, but rather if it should be done internally, or if it should be outsourced. Of course, several checks you will need to complete can't be done in-house, such as criminal record and credit checks, but many checks can be.

Those who advocate for handling the screenings internally seem to be looking at the problem from a budget perspective. Don't you save money by checking certain things yourself? Not if you look at the big picture. In fact, there are so many other problems that doing your own background checks can introduce.

For example, one of our clients at BMP initially had students assist in conducting social media checks on potential candidates. They quickly realized this was a mistake when the students saw too much personal and confidential information. They brought this important task back to the hiring manager's team and soon, they realized how time-consuming that was, because it is so easy to go down that social media rabbit hole.

Once they started outsourcing these checks to the BMP team, their own hiring team only spent their time on LinkedIn. They were using LinkedIn as a recruitment tool but staying away from all other social media platforms. As a result, they were able to find better qualified candidates in a shorter period of time.

Outsourcing certain background checks—especially social media checks—to professionals can make the process quicker and more thorough and, more importantly, it ensures objective reviews.

When conducting your own checks, it actively feeds the human capacity for bias. While looking for specific information in your search, you may end up exposed to other classes of information that should be irrelevant to your hiring decision and, in fact, may bias it. This is especially true in terms of social media checks. Yet, you can't unsee something once you've seen it—it now consciously, or subconsciously, becomes a factor in your decision-making process. A prejudiced team is the enemy of good hiring.

There is also the risk of doing your check to the extent possible with the tools you have, then having yourself believe that you've hired a candidate you can trust when, in fact, you haven't. You likely don't have access to the technology that can make the screening process go faster and be more thorough. BMP uses state-of-the-art technology and access to hundreds of databases that, for example, allow for our social media checks to be completed quickly and thoroughly.

No background check is made better if you're rushed. You don't have the time to commit to doing the task well. By outsourcing certain tasks to a third party, especially to one who has access to software that will make the task more efficient, you can focus on other tasks that are a better use of your time. By outsourcing, you're doing yourself a favour. If you're in a hurry, you may end up caving to that pressure and only scratch the surface in your screening process. It's important to do the job properly.

In addition, if you start assuming the role of an investigator yourself, you will find that most information is not easily available to the public. An example of this would be criminal record checks. In Canada and many other countries, criminal record information can only come directly from the police services. Employers don't have access to this information; they would have to outsource this to a third party. In the United States, criminal record information is more public and it's easy to waste hours searching databases, only to not be completely certain if the information you are looking at is for the correct person.

Another concern with doing your own background check as opposed to hiring a professional to do it is the risk of not finding information that you should have found. What if one of your clients does a quick Google search on an employee and finds information you should have found, such as involvement in a scandal that made the news or went viral, or adverse or objectionable content on their social media? That client will wonder why your company didn't do the same search. Why did you hire this person? If you know about their background, what have you done to ensure they won't engage in similar behaviour again? Do you maybe hold the same values and beliefs as your employee? And how do your other employees feel about it?

Outsourcing background checks can also potentially assist in avoiding a potential lawsuit. It can get very messy playing the detective role. Are you looking at the right person? Have you created a rubric that is fair and consistent for everyone? And are you abiding by the relevant privacy and data protection laws?

Use the resources that are available to you, and partner with companies that have access to the tools and technology to ensure that you are being compliant in your hiring process and that you do, in fact, know the person you want to hire.

There is a duty of care that consumers and the general public expect companies to take in today's world, and efficiently screening candidates or employees is one of them.

Protected Class Information

A protected class or a protected group is one protected by anti-discrimination laws. What these groups are depends on the country, but they can include women, older people, people with disabilities, certain ethnic groups and minorities; and can consider gender, marital status, religion, sexual orientation, pregnancy, and even HIV/AIDS status. Anti-discrimination laws aim to ensure equality and prevent discrimination in many areas, but mostly for housing and employment purposes.

Before any type of background check can be processed, a potential candidate must give written permission, which is usually done by signing a consent form. An individual does have the right to say no to this check; however, it may limit their ability to move through the hiring process.

These protected classes are enforced by bodies such as human rights tribunals or commissions at both the federal and provincial or state levels. Individuals who experience discrimination based on any of the protected classes can file a complaint with the relevant office. The process will involve some type of investigation to determine if the case is accurate and justified. Depending on the outcome, a person may receive some sort of compensation or reinstatement. A company may also have to show proof of implementing policies or practices to prevent future discrimination.

A background-checking company's job is to ensure our clients know who they are hiring. Hence, we are required to gather a great deal of information on a potential candidate. By outsourcing the pre-employment screening part to a third party, a potential employer does not have access to a lot of the personal and confidential information about a potential candidate, until the person is hired. This allows for a company to be more objective, since they have no preconceived ideas on who they are hiring.

However, we've also seen some employers use the background report to exclude candidates who have a criminal record, or based on race, national origin, or other protected characteristics. This is one of the reasons that a hiring team or recruiter must remain objective. A third party helps ensure objectivity because they will typically redact protected class information from the report they submit to you. That way, you can remain fair in your hiring.

Making the Best Decision for Your Business

By now, you understand the importance of a thorough, well-rounded evaluation to find candidates that truly fit your organization's needs, both today and into the future. However, no matter how meticulous your process is, making the final hiring decision is still complicated, with many factors to consider. This is where partnering with an expert background-screening firm can provide enormous value.

Partnering with experts takes the guesswork out of ensuring you're making the safest choice. Their screening standards and processes are written by legal and HR compliance specialists to fully adhere to the guidelines of the Employment Equity Act in Canada, or similar legislation in other countries. You can have peace of mind that selecting a candidate who passes their screening puts you on solid legal ground.

In the end, you need to feel confident in your hiring choices. By leveraging the skills of a background-screening expert, you gain an extra set of objective eyes protecting your business interests while maintaining fairness for applicants. Don't leave such an important responsibility to chance—make verification by an expert a vital step for every hire.

Section 3:
Practical Steps for
the Hiring Manager

Chapter 8:
Your Background-checking Checklist

Everyone loves checklists. Up until now, we have only been talking about background checks as an umbrella term without getting into its components. Now it's time to dig deep. What different types are there, or what is housed under such a broad concept?

When you want to hire the right person the first time, there is a broad range of screenings to conduct. A lot of these will require the consent of the candidate.

You don't necessarily need to do every type of check for every job—the checks you'll require depend on factors such as the seniority level of the position, the kind of responsibilities the job requires, the kind of information or resources the candidate will be handling or have access to, the industry, and the candidate's country of origin.

In addition, checks should not only be done at the onboarding stage. The BMP team has a few clients who recheck all their employees' criminal records and driver abstracts on an annual basis to ensure that no one on their team has had any convictions or driving infractions during their employment with the company.

A comprehensive background check can include the following:

Quality reference checks. Reference checks are a very good indicator of how a candidate will or will not perform for you, so they're recommended for every job, including entry-level positions. If the candidate has no job experience—for example, if they're a recent graduate—they may provide references from a teacher or professor, a coach, a guidance counsellor, or anyone who acted in a leadership capacity towards them, such as a faith leader or the leader of a club the candidate may belong to.

Some companies will conduct reference checks electronically by sending a list of questions to the reference. The BMP team does not recommend such methods of reference checking for our client base. If you conduct the reference by making a phone call, there are several probing questions to ensure the person is a qualified reference. We will discuss this in more detail in Chapter 9.

Employment verifications. An employment verification is recommended for every kind of job where the candidate has some work experience, since it shows the applicant's work history. The employment verification will look at each job they've listed on their resume and verify their job title, dates of employment, and reason for leaving. People don't want to show gaps on their resumes, so they often stretch the dates of employment. People also tend to polish their job titles, and it's difficult to know when they have crossed a line into providing information that is fraudulent. Chapter 10 takes a closer look at how to verify a candidate's employment history.

Education verifications. Education verifications are useful for any kind of job that requires a certain level of education and/or a specific type of qualification, such as a bachelor's degree in marketing. After all, the candidate's level of education often helps determine their level of seniority and their salary, particularly in the case of full-time positions. It's especially important to verify the person's education when they work in a profession that can have a profound impact on someone else's life, such as healthcare or law.

It's critical that you always verify a potential candidate's education through the actual institution or a repository that confirms this information on their behalf. Within this sphere, we also check any professional designation, and that all licensing and professional qualifications are up to date and factual, so in some cases, we'll do education verification checks annually instead of only during the onboarding stage. We expand on education verifications in Chapter 11.

Criminal record checks. Before 9/11, criminal record checks were not a commonly run check as part of the onboarding for a new employee. After 9/11, companies started to implement conducting a criminal record check as part of their recruitment process, and today there are not too many jobs you apply for where you'll not be required to have at least a basic criminal record check done.

A candidate who will be working with vulnerable people such as children, the elderly, or disabled people may also be subject to a vulnerability sector check, which is a more in-depth check looking for very specific information. Chapter 12 has more on conducting criminal record checks.

Credit checks. When onboarding an employee who will be working as part of your finance team, it's recommended that you conduct a credit check. You don't want someone with a history of poor management to have access to large sums of money. Credit bureaus will provide valuable information on a person's credit score, show slow payments, bankruptcies, and other important information. We go into more detail about credit checks in Chapter 13.

Identity verifications. Identity verification is the process of confirming or denying that a claimed identity is correct by comparing the credentials with the identity being claimed. When COVID hit, we saw an increase in identity verifications, since remote hiring became the norm and continues to be more commonplace. You always want to know exactly who you're hiring, but it can be even trickier when you may never meet the candidate in person—either before or after the hiring process. The technology used to identify a person has been constantly evolving. Chapter 14 discusses identity verifications in more detail.

Additional checks. Depending on the job, the company, and the industry, there are additional checks that you may want to perform. These include global sanctions checks, driving record checks, and immunization checks.

A global sanctions check is important when candidates are moving around globally or when you're hiring internationally. If you have employees driving company vehicles, you should process an annual or even semi-annual driving record check to ensure that each employee maintains a clean record.

Immunization checks are mostly for the healthcare and pharmaceutical industries, but they may be required for other jobs too. Someone who works with animals, for example, may be required to have been vaccinated against rabies, hepatitis B, tetanus, and even influenza, which will reduce the risk of catching swine flu or avian flu.

These additional checks are covered in Chapter 15.

Exit and retention interviews. These interviews can help to maintain a positive workplace culture and are recommended for all positions. Having a third party, like BMP, conduct these interviews also adds value, since the person being interviewed is more likely to open up to a third party. You can find out more about exit and retention interviews in Chapter 16.

Social media checks. It is highly recommended to conduct social media checks on all your employees. This can be done while onboarding and beyond, throughout employment. This is a large topic and one you will want to be particularly careful with, and we cover it extensively in Section 4 of this book.

Privacy and Data Protection Legislation

When you screen potential or current employees, no matter for what position, it's very important to comply with privacy and data protection legislation. The specifics of these laws may vary from country to country, and even at provincial or state level.

With the rise of remote hiring, many companies have changed their hiring practices. One of our clients, for whom we provide pre-employment screening services in Canada, was delighted to be hiring an employee who lived in India. In order to ensure the proper due diligence was completed so that our client had peace of mind, the BMP team had to first find out about the privacy and data protection laws that apply in India.

If you regularly hire employees from a certain country, you will save time and money if you get acquainted with that country's privacy and data protection laws, on both a national and provincial or state level. Here's a breakdown of the legislation to know about in Canada, the United States, the European Union, and the United Kingdom.

Canada

In Canada, employers must adhere to the *Personal Information Protection and Electronic Documents Act*, or PIPEDA. Every business and federally regulated organization that operates in Canada and handles personal information across provincial or national borders in the course of their commercial activity is subject to PIPEDA. Even when the business is based in a province or territory with its own legislation that's similar to

PIPEDA, the business must still adhere to PIPEDA too. The only exceptions are British Columbia, Alberta, and Quebec, and only when the business operates entirely within the borders of that province, where provincial privacy laws apply. As soon as they do business across their provincial borders, PIPEDA applies.

PIPEDA defines commercial activity as: "any particular transaction, act or conduct or any regular course of conduct that is of a commercial character, including the selling, bartering or leasing of donor, membership or other fundraising lists."

The United States

The United States doesn't have an overarching privacy and data protection law. Instead, there are different laws to regulate different kinds of data. Federal laws to be aware of include the following:

- The *Privacy Act*: Because of this law, agencies need the person's written permission before they can disclose their personal information to anyone else. There are some exceptions, but these are usually more related to using the data for statistical purposes.
- The *Gramm-Leach-Bliley Act*, or GLBA: This law regulates how financial institutions collect, protect, and share their customers' information. It doesn't prohibit the sharing of customers' information, but it requires the institution to notify the customer and to give them an opportunity to opt out of having their information shared.

- The *Fair Credit Reporting Act*, or FCRA: This law regulates how consumer reporting agencies such as credit bureaus, medical information companies, and tenant screening services must collect, disseminate, and use consumer credit information. The act specifies who the information in a consumer report can be provided to, and for what purpose. In addition, when a company that uses the information for credit, insurance, or employment purposes takes an adverse action because of the information they receive, they must notify the consumer.

In addition to the different federal laws that protect privacy and personal data, there are state laws to adhere to as well. California, for instance, has strict privacy laws.

The European Union

The European Union has a particularly strong privacy law for properly storing the personal information. It's called the *General Data Protection Regulation*, or GDPR, and has been in effect since 2018. It applies to anyone, anywhere in the world, who collects data about people in the European Union.

The GDPR outlines seven principles you must comply with when processing data:

1. You must process the data in a way that is within the law, fair, and transparent to the person whose data you're collecting.
2. You must explicitly specify to the person why you are collecting the data.

3. You should not collect any more data than what is absolutely necessary for the purposes that you've specified.

4. You must keep any personal data up to date and accurate.

5. You may store the data you collected and that is personally identifying, only for as long as necessary for the purpose that you've specified.

6. You must process the data in a way that ensures it will remain secure and confidential. For example, you can use encryption to protect it.

7. It is the data controller's responsibility to be able to show compliance with all of the principles of the GDPR.

In addition to the GDPR, member countries of the European Union may have specific legislation, such as anti-discrimination laws, to be mindful of too.

The United Kingdom

The United Kingdom has its own version of the GDPR that is used in the European Union. It's called the *Data Protection Act* and is based on the same seven principles.

In addition, there are other laws to be mindful of, depending on the information you're looking for. These include:

- The *Equality Act*: This is an anti-discrimination law that outlines what is and isn't admissible when the candidate is a member of a protected class.

- The *Rehabilitation of Offenders Act*: This law, along with its accompanying Exceptions Order, outlines which criminal convictions a job applicant needs to declare and how employers may conduct criminal record checks.

Chapter 9:
Reference Checks

This is the focus area that birthed our company all the way back in 1974. Investigative reference checking was all we did in those days. We had managed to build a system that ensured we obtained as accurate information in as short a time as possible, when no one else was doing it. The process did take longer than it does today. References were not provided to the BMP team by the client or the candidate; we had to source them on our own. We would do this by calling the company where the candidate used to work and ask to speak with someone in the personnel department. We would then ask who the best person would be to provide a reference for the candidate.

This form of reference checking was a real art. It brought great value to our clients in assisting them to understand who they were hiring! Our reputation grew quickly as the first to offer such a service and produce quality results. Our clients had confidence in the BMP team.

To get the best out of a reference check, you will need to consider the kind of information that you want to obtain, how you're going to go about getting that information, and who you are going to contact. Obviously, consent and permission are required.

Reference checking has evolved over time, along with changes in technology, communication methods, and the job market. Here are some of the favoured ways for checking a reference— some more effective than others.

Phone and Video Calls

BMP still considers phone and video calls the most effective way to conduct thorough reference checks, especially for executive-type positions. As more people are working remotely and global workforces are becoming the norm, conducting traditional reference checks via telephone can have its challenges and become more expensive. As a result, we've used tools like Zoom to improve the live reference-checks process.

Having an actual conversation is important for several reasons. It provides the opportunity to listen to what is not being said— trust me, that is a real art today. Also, knowing when to probe deeper and ask clarifying questions adds a tremendous advantage to the quality of the information that you will obtain. So does having the ability to customize the reference-check questions. Our clients will come to us with specific questions or concerns that they may have picked up in the interview process and ask us to probe deeply into these areas. Most importantly, it provides us the opportunity to verify the identity of the reference and ensure it is a legitimate source of information.

What is our focus in a call?

We listen to a reference's tone and ask clarifying questions. We have structured questions on hand that are customized to the position that the candidate is applying for. For example, if the candidate is applying for a sales position, we focus on determining if the candidate has the skillset our client requires. Also, we are ready to follow up on new angles that come up on the fly. We ask the reference about the candidate's skills, work ethic, and qualifications, and then we check that these match what the candidate listed on their resume.

It's important to be discerning, and this comes with years of experience on the job. We are able to ask the right follow-up questions and know how to listen well. Our team listens for the hesitations and to what is not being said. Truthful responses typically come more quickly.

It is also important to establish a good rapport with the person. Once there is a connection, it's easier to get the person to open up. Because we're trying to fit in the schedules of the references, the process can have some back and forth, and even when we fix the best time for the call, we need to build up the environment of the call to be just right. We want the reference to be comfortable, because we need them to be forthcoming.

We are calling to get information, and to get it, we need to be polite, respectful, flexible, and likeable.

It's important to ask for examples. We probe deep, and we continue to clarify if there is something we don't understand. If we find the person we are speaking with is losing interest and wants to end the call as soon as possible, we adjust the order of our questions, and ask the most important ones first.

We try to make sure not to get off the call before discussing what the reference thinks are the potential areas of development for the candidate. While it's a critical question, it's not one we include in the first few questions we ask. It's best to keep it for later in the interview process. It's not likely someone is going to answer that question honestly until you've established a good rapport with them.

So, it is not merely about nailing the list of questions, but also knowing the best timing for each one.

Despite this seemingly arduous process, an in-person call remains the best way to gather information about how a candidate will perform for you. We measure this in terms of the quality of information you can get. With other methods, you may get answers, tick the reference-check box as having been done, but you really haven't given yourself any range to measure the veracity of the information before you. In some ways, you will have created another document that still needs as much verifying as the resume you're verifying!

Sometimes, a client will come to us with a rush request. They tell us that a candidate has another job offer. They don't believe there is time to wait through the background-screening process. We understand the primary issues that come up in these situations. We can't speed up the process if it means not being thorough. Our business relies heavily on doing quality work and having new customers referred to us by our existing ones. Word of mouth is still the best way to grow a business.

For example, one of our BMP associates conducted a reference check on a high-level executive. The reference we contacted initially did not have much time to speak with us, but after a few moments of friendly banter and quickly determining a personal interest with them, the reference-check interview ended up going much longer than our associate required, and the openness of the referee was incredible. Valuable information was obtained for our client. In fact, because of the relationship established during our reference-checking call, BMP developed a new client. They were impressed by the quality of the process and realized how valuable a properly conducted reference check can be.

However, if we make the client wait too long for a thorough reference check, then it is more likely their candidate will accept another job, and that is not what any employer wants when they believe they have found great talent. So, we seek a middle-ground in this situation, and it's usually that the client should consider giving the candidate a conditional offer pending the successful completion of the entire background check.

Structured Questionnaires

As companies grew and hiring processes became more standardized, structured reference-check questionnaires started to be used for reference checks. Instead of relying solely on structured phone conversations, reference checkers would work with our clients to customize questionnaire templates to gather specific information about the candidate's performance and qualifications. For example, the BMP team would add customized sales questions for a sales role: Did they meet their sales goals? How were their customer relations? For hiring in an accounting position, you would want to focus on their financial acumen.

Lately, there has undoubtedly been an increase in the number of these email-based references being completed. Businesses are looking for ways to cut expenses and speed up turnaround times. With this move towards questionnaires, however, reference checking can lose quality.

Besides email, online reference-checking software has also emerged over the years, and they, too, typically use structured questionnaires. Online platforms have been developed to offer these services.

However, there are significant drawbacks to both methods. Our concern is knowing who the person is. In an email response, you can't listen to the hesitations in a person's voice and don't have the ability to probe with clarifying questions. The probing part is where you get the important information that is so valuable.

It's also a challenge when a candidate provides a reference who is not responsive or willing to cooperate. Besides causing more work for the reference checkers, it could raise some doubts about the candidate's credibility.

At BMP, we had a case where the client provided our team

with a list of three references. Only email addresses were provided. We reached out to our client to ask permission to conduct the references via email, since it was not their policy to do so. The client did not want us to contact the references via email. We then asked the candidate to provide us with phone numbers. The candidate was not very cooperative. When we finally reached out to the three references, they appeared to be the same person, with similarities in their tone of voice and the manner in which they spoke. We advised our client that we were concerned with the legitimacy of the references and suddenly, the candidate withdrew from the interview process.

There are pros and cons to each type of reference check, in-person or electronic. You must decide what is important to you and which method you prefer.

Case Study

In the United Kingdom, there was a case where an airline pilot provided a fake reference when applying for a job with a cargo airline, and the airline gave him the job as well as training, based on what he said his previous experience had been.

As reported in *People Management*, when the airline discovered the lie, they gave the pilot the option of resigning with immediate effect. He did, but then brought an Employment Tribunal claim for the three months' notice pay he was contractually entitled to. The airline brought a counterclaim for the costs of training him. The Employment Tribunal dismissed the pilot's claim and found in favour of the airline's claim, awarding them £4,725.

What makes this case particularly memorable is that the airline could have avoided all of this, as well as potential liability if the pilot had crashed one of their planes, if they had simply googled the reference's name. The name that the pilot had provided was Desilijic Tiure, which *Star Wars* fans might recognize as part of the full name of Jabba the Hutt.

Chapter 10:
Employment Verifications

As BMP started to become known as reference-checking experts and established a good reputation in the industry, we added new types of checks to our list of services. Deciding on what to add typically came from changes that we saw within the industry, or a request from a client. Employment verifications were the first service offering we added.

Employment verification is the process of confirming a person's past work history. This typically helps confirm the accuracy of their job history and employment details from their past employer, their title while employed at that company, and dates of employment. If the candidate is no longer employed with the company, their reason for leaving that company is important to know: particularly, was it voluntary or not, and if it wasn't, what was the reason why they had to leave that job?

You must be on high alert here and cover all the ground that you can, even if the person was employed in the most bureaucratic organization on Earth, where you are redirected to twelve people before you speak to the right one. You want to be sure your candidate has been honest, so that you can see if they are actually as fit for the job as they seem to be on paper. We have found that this is an area where candidates will typically misrepresent themselves. The job description that has been posted has told them what you're looking for, so they can decide to simply tell you what you want to hear. This makes this type of check critical before you hire for a role that's valuable to your company.

Our purpose for conducting an employment verification is mostly for employment purposes. However, there are also many other reasons that an employment verification is completed. These include applying for a loan, mortgage, or credit card.

When the employment verification is being conducted for employment, it's important to confirm that the candidate did what they said they did and has the skillset required for the new employment opportunity. When an individual applies for a new job, the prospective employer should always request employment verifications to ensure that the information provided on the resume or application is accurate. This will also assist the potential employer in knowing whether the person has the right skills for the job and would fit with the company.

With the rise of the gig economy, there has emerged a "new" difficulty in verifying employment. Verification of self-employment or freelance work can be more challenging than verification of traditional employment, since there are likely fewer formal records to consult.

While we find that most of the misrepresentation comes from dates of employment—often to hide gaps in employment history—and job title, reasons for leaving the employer can also differ between employee and employer. A candidate is unlikely to be completely honest about having been fired from a job for a serious offence, so employment verification will help you get the full story.

We've seen cases where a candidate will add false employers to their resume. They may even tell you that the company they were formally employed with no longer exists, hence making the verification of some employment extremely difficult and time-consuming. In cases like these, it may be helpful to ask for pay stubs or confirmation from previous tax returns, with all confidential information redacted in order to comply with privacy and data protection laws.

Case Study

In April 2019, former pop singer Mina Chang got the job of Deputy Assistant Secretary in the Bureau of Conflict and Stabilization Operations of the United States Department of State. To take this job, she resigned as president and CEO of a non-profit. There was even speculation that she could become the next United States Ambassador to the Philippines.

But then *NBC News* did some digging— the digging that her employer should have done about her employment history—and in November of that year, they published their findings. She had misrepresented her qualifications, using words like "alumna" and "graduate" to imply she was more qualified than she was. In addition, she had falsely claimed she had served on a United Nations panel, had testified before Congress, and had addressed both the Republican and Democratic national conventions three years earlier. She had even brought a fake *Time* magazine cover with her face on it to an interview and didn't correct the interviewer when they assumed the cover was real.

Six days after the *NBC News* article appeared, Chang resigned from her job.

The controversy not only caused embarrassment to her employer, but also had an impact on the non-profit where she used to work: once the *NBC News* article appeared, they removed the video of her interview featuring the fake *Time* magazine cover and the "donate" button from their website.

The BMP team has several partners that provide us with access to a variety of databases that increase our likelihood of verifying information that is typically difficult to verify. Such repositories are big business in the background-screening world. More companies come into the market every day. Some companies and institutions have an agreement with a third-party verification service, and the only way you'll be able to obtain the information you require is by going through their systems, which often involves paying a fee.

Whenever possible, we attempt to obtain the verifications directly from the source—the company the candidate worked for. Our clients continue to use BMP to collect the confirmations, because it's usually part of an entire background-check package. Otherwise, the client would require an account with each of the repositories, resulting in a tedious process.

Consent must be provided by the candidate before we can contact a current employer to conduct an employment verification. Once we have that, we will obtain:

- Dates of employment (start and end dates)
- Job titles and responsibilities
- Salary or compensation information
- Verification of any awards or achievements
- Whether the individual is eligible for rehire
- Other relevant details about the employment relationship

When employers respond, it's important that both employers and individuals are honest and accurate in providing and verifying employment information, as misrepresentations can have legal and professional consequences.

Chapter 11:
Education Verifications

Education checks, as with employment verifications, have become increasingly important over the decades. Implementing a robust educational verification check process within a company is a first line of defence against fraud. Early detection of fraudulent claims will assist in protecting a company from potential harm.

But procuring the data can be a very time-consuming process. Certain repositories control the data, which means more fees to access the information.

Educational repositories are online storage systems that allow confirmation of academic credentials. We've also seen a rise in online platforms used by employers, education providers, and government agencies around the world to verify the authenticity of educational credentials, transcripts, and other academic records online.

Often, when our Canadian clients are hiring employees who were educated outside of North America, the process is more complicated and costly, especially when documents need to be translated or authenticated. The amount of time this can take varies, depending on factors such as the record-keeping systems they use—especially with older candidates, their records may still be in paper form—as well as whether the institution is understaffed or not, or simply how responsive they are in general. Turnaround time for an education verification can be a concern when an employer needs to onboard an employee in a timely manner. When this happens and we see a delay with the international educational confirmation, we advise some of our clients to put in a conditional employment offer pending the clearance of the successful education check.

It's unfortunate when all the hard work and time it takes to find the right candidate results in an unsuccessful hire due to unsubstantiated education checks. But it does happen, and it's better to catch it before determining it later in the hiring process, after you've spent a substantial amount of money to onboard an employee.

People now have the resources to create fraudulent degrees. Since we are typically not seeing the original copy of a degree, and for the most part only a digital version, we have received forged versions. For example, the BMP team once had a candidate with a degree from a Canadian university. The candidate was asked to provide a copy. Once received, we sent the degree to the university to verify the document. It looked authentic. But fonts were different, alignment of the text was incorrect, and there were even simple errors. The institution was extremely upset and took legal action against the candidate. As a result, the candidate now has a criminal charge on their record.

When you receive a copy of a candidate's degree, diploma, or certificate, one way to verify its authenticity is to compare it to a real degree from the same school, paying close attention to the font choices or signatures and seals.

It's important to verify educational credentials to ensure a level of trust and credibility. So it's important to be sure. It will also ensure they have the necessary qualifications and skills that are required for the job that they are applying for.

It's also important to verify educational qualifications to ensure compliance with legal and industry standards. For example, in some professions and industries, there are legal and regulatory requirements to confirm the verification of educational qualifications. These may include but are not limited to finance, healthcare, and education.

Preventing fraud and misrepresentation is critical for the success of an organization. Bringing an employee into an organization who does not have the skills required to do the job could pose serious risks to the company, especially when a specialized skillset is required. By conducting the proper background-check processes, you can eliminate this at the start.

However, it's also important to conduct an annual re-checking process to ensure any existing employee credentials have not expired. If you've onboarded a professional engineer, for example, you should verify on an annual basis that the person is still a member of their professional engineering association. The BMP team has a number of clients who validate the renewal of their employees' credentials on an annual basis.

The verifications will also assist with fairness in the hiring process. They eliminate a candidate gaining an unfair advantage by claiming false qualifications.

Case Study

According to *Global News*, in 2019 the Quebec College of Physicians issued a warning to its members that there was a woman pretending to be a doctor, even though she had no relevant medical training. She would gain access to a hospital and get to see patients by wearing a white lab coat and a stethoscope.

The woman claimed to be a medical resident at a hospital in Montreal. Based on her supposed training, two clinics gave her internships.

The College announced that they were pursuing legal action. Still, two qualified people missed out on internships because the clinics in question didn't verify the qualifications of the woman who got those internships instead.

It's important as well to verify the educational backgrounds of any researchers or collaborators you may bring into your company to assist on special projects. Even if that person will only be with you for a short period of time, if their name will be associated with any work they are doing for you, again, it's important to verify their educational credentials. You would not want it to reflect badly on the company later that a person was not qualified for the job they were hired to do.

Not only is it a mandatory requirement that an employer verify a potential employee's academic qualifications, but it's also important to verify that the institution that qualified them is indeed legitimate. There are more and more bogus academic institutions offering academic credentials to individuals at a cost. Take the time and do your homework to ensure the institution that you are considering is indeed accredited and reputable. Some ways to do this include:

- Check with whichever body regulates academic institutions in that country, such as a national and provincial education department, whether the institution is accredited with them. An accredited academic institution usually indicates on their website who they're accredited with, so you can use this as a starting point.

- While this generally isn't true in the case of Canada and some European countries, accredited academic institutions in other countries often contain either a .edu or a .ac in their domain name. For example, the domain name for Harvard University is www.harvard.edu, while Sydney University in Australia has the domain name www.sydney.edu.au. The University of Oxford in the United Kingdom uses the domain name www.ox.ac.uk.

- Google Maps and Google Street View are handy tools for checking the institution's physical address to see if it actually exists. Make sure though that the name you have corresponds with the name on the map or on Street View images, because some bogus institutions will list the physical address of a real, accredited institution.
- Use LinkedIn to see if you can find past students or faculty. In the case of faculty, you can usually also find academic papers they have published.

Chapter 12:
Criminal Record Checks

As an employer, it is your responsibility to do what you reasonably can to ensure that your current employees and customers will be safe, and that starts by ensuring the new people you hire are who they say they are and have the skills and training they say they do. If one of your employees becomes violent, or does something illegal, your company could be guilty of negligent hiring and held liable for damages.

The laws around negligent hiring got their start in the early 1900s in the United States. The *Federal Employers' Liability Act* was introduced in 1906 in the United States. It's widely reported in the background-screening industry that one of the precursors to this law was an employer who kept an apprentice on the job even after they pulled a prank that resulted in the death of a coworker. Over the next few decades, a series of amendments were enacted that covered acts that occurred outside of employment. In 1951, after a delivery man attacked a housewife, the courts found the employer responsible, as they hadn't done their due diligence in hiring a reputable employee. By the late 1970s, more employers were being prosecuted in cases such as this. This, in turn, forced companies to take background screening during hiring more seriously. My father's timing—launching a background-checking company in 1974—was excellent.

Even so, the practice of an employer conducting a criminal record check on a potential employee was not that common. It tended to only be done in certain sectors or for particular roles, for example positions of trust with vulnerable populations, such as children. After the 9/11 attacks, people lost trust in one another, including in the workplace, and the need arose to understand who was being hired and what risks might be associated with hiring them.

In Canada, the landscape shifted once again with the advent of Bill 113, *Police Record Check Reform Act*. This act defined a structure for running background checks in a safe and respectful way. Criminal background checks have since gained traction in unprecedented ways.

Criminal record checks are now easily the most common check conducted. They assist companies in determining if a potential employee has been charged or convicted of a crime that may be relevant to the role they will hold. A history of breaking the law can be a red flag for a company looking to hire someone they will need to trust with company information and resources.

However, the process isn't about trying to exclude everyone with any kind of criminal record, but rather about gathering enough information to make a balanced decision based on the potential risks. When the results came back from a criminal record check that was conducted for one of our Canadian clients, we flagged it as a caution because the candidate had a marijuana charge from the early 1980s. The client asked us why we flagged the report as a warning if marijuana was now legal in Canada. We indicated that at the time of the arrest, marijuana *was* illegal in Canada, hence the report remained included.

The team at BMP mostly conducts criminal record checks for employment purposes. However, they can also be requested for volunteer work, citizenship, adoption, student/intern placements, housing, as well as international travel. In some cases, the presence of a record can pose difficulties in obtaining a professional licence. They can also prevent a person from sponsoring someone to gain a Canadian visa, as well as emigrating to another country.

The process of checking if a person has a criminal record is typically started with a name and date-of-birth search. If this is not a definite way to confirm a person's identity, the use of fingerprints is the most accurate way to verify. It was in the early 1900s that fingerprinting started to be used as a means of identifying criminals. When conducting a criminal record check, this is the only way to confirm the accuracy of the information. If someone with the same name and date of birth as a candidate has a criminal record, they may be asked to have fingerprints processed. In addition, since 2013, travellers, students, and workers from certain visa-required countries and territories are required to provide fingerprints and have their photo taken before they arrive in Canada.

Criminal record checks are subject to the privacy and data protection laws that apply in the province or state and the country that you do business in and where the candidate lives. These laws regulate what is permissible for background checks in the public sector and have been discussed in Chapter 8. In Canada, we must abide by the privacy policies in PIPEDA. In the United States, our criminal record checks must adhere to the *Freedom of Information Act*, or FOIA, and the *Privacy Act*. Any checks conducted in the European Union must adhere to the GDPR, while in the United Kingdom, the laws regulating what you can and can't check in terms of criminal records are the *Data Protection Act* and the *Rehabilitation of Offenders Act*.

The Different Criminal Record Checks

In Canada, there are different types of police record checks that can be obtained through the RCMP. For employment and volunteer purposes, the type of information released depends on the type of job the person is applying for, whether it's in the public or private sector, and if it's for the public sector, whether it's for the federal government, the provincial government, or the RCMP.

It's important to know that the criminal-record check process may vary by province. For example, there are three main types of police record check in Ontario:

1. **Criminal record check:** A basic criminal record check looks for any evidence of being charged or convicted of a crime.

2. **Criminal record and judicial matters check:** This takes the basic criminal record check a step further, to verify if the candidate has any outstanding warrants, charges, or judicial orders on top of being charged or convicted.

3. **Vulnerable sector check:** This check goes even deeper than the criminal record and judicial matters check, to include cases where the person was found to be not criminally responsible due to mental disorder, has record suspensions for sexual offences, or has been charged with but not convicted of certain other offences, subject to strict criteria. This kind of check is commonly done for nurses, caregivers, and others who work with vulnerable people such as children, the elderly, or people with disabilities.

Once a record suspension has been granted, the individual's criminal record check will come back as clear, with no convictions found, except in the case of sexual offences. Once a person has served their time and has proven to be a law-abiding citizen, they can apply for and be granted a record suspension.

Laws and policies surrounding criminal record checks may change over time, so it's important to stay in the know with the latest legislation surrounding Canadian criminal record checks.

In the United States, criminal record information is considered public record and the systems to obtain the data are far more evolved than in Canada.

Internationally, criminal record checks vary significantly on a country-to-country basis and in many cases, criminal records may not be legally accessible for employment purposes. The team at BMP is fortunate to work with an international provider who has the ability to process our criminal record checks on a global level, while ensuring we are compliant on any check we process.

Chapter 13:
Credit Checks

BMP once had a client who had invested a great deal of time to recruit a senior executive in finance. We spent time processing many checks for the client, which included references, education, employment, even a social media check. As the recruitment process was winding down and the client was getting ready to make an offer, at the very last minute the client decided they wanted to conduct a credit report. BMP ordered the credit check, and it came back with bankruptcies. If the client had done this inexpensive check at the very beginning of the recruitment process, they would have saved valuable time and money.

If you are hiring anyone to work in a finance-related position, it's important to be aware of their own financial situation. After all, how could you trust someone to work with your company's finances if they can't manage their own? This is why you should consider ordering a credit report through credit bureaus.

I'm sure you're aware of this, but a credit report is a detailed record of a person's or an entity's credit history and financial activities. It's used by lenders, creditors, landlords, and other financial institutions to assess the creditworthiness of a person or a business when making a lending or financial decision. It's maintained by the credit reporting agencies, which are also referred to as credit bureaus.

A credit bureau is a company that collects and compiles information regarding a person's credit history from banks, other financial institutions, and various other bodies such as courthouses and Canada's Office of the Superintendent of Bankruptcy, the United States Trustee Program, or whichever body is responsible for the administration of bankruptcy cases in other countries.

Of course, permission is always required from the candidate before this type of check can be ordered. Personal information, such as name, address, date of birth, as well as a social insurance number in Canada or social security number in the United States are required.

Once permission is received from the candidate, processing a credit report only takes a few minutes and the results are instantaneous. It is wise to review the report carefully to ensure a data entry error was not made when ordering the report. There is also a fee associated with ordering a credit report, so it's important to enter the correct information the first time. If not, you'll be charged each time you order the report. Also, it's important to review the accuracy of the information provided by the credit bureau. Cross-reference name, address, date of birth, and all personal information in the system to ensure accuracy.

A credit report contains a great deal of confidential and personal information, so it's recommended that only trusted sources save access to the results. It's extremely important to safeguard and provide limited access to this information.

A typical credit report includes the following key components:

- **Personal information.** This section includes name, current and previous addresses, social insurance number or equivalent national ID, date of birth, and employment history.

- **Credit accounts.** This section lists all open and closed credit accounts, including credit cards, loans, mortgages, and other forms of credit. It provides information on the creditor, account number, type of credit, credit limit or loan amount, outstanding balance, and payment history.

- **Payment history.** This is one of the most critical parts of the credit report. It shows whether payments were made on time, and whether any payments were missed or late payments existed in the past. In terms of late payments, it will typically show payments over thirty, sixty, or ninety days past due. Late or missed payments can have a negative impact on a credit score.

- **Public records.** This section includes information about any bankruptcies, tax liens, or any judgements against a person. These negative public records can significantly impact creditworthiness.

- **Inquiries.** This lists all the inquiries made on a credit report. There are two types of inquiries: Soft inquiries are typically from lenders or companies conducting background checks for pre-approval offers, and hard inquiries result from credit applications. Many hard inquiries in a short period can negatively affect a credit score.

- **Collections.** If there are accounts that have been sent to collections due to unpaid debts, this information will be reported in this section.

- **Credit score.** Some credit reports include a credit score, which is a numerical representation of creditworthiness based on the information in the credit report. FICO and VantageScore are commonly used credit scoring models.

How Do FICO Scores Work?

A FICO score is a single number consisting of three digits. It measures a credit situation and shows lenders what kind of risk the borrower presents. Each lender will decide for themselves what they consider a poor score and what is a good score, but typically, a FICO score of below 580 is considered a poor score, while a score above 800 is considered exceptional. Lenders generally believe that a FICO score of over 680 indicates good creditworthiness.

Financial institutions rely heavily on this score for loans, approval of mortgages, and the interest rate that someone qualifies for. A FICO score is based on the following:

- **Payment history.** About 35 per cent of each FICO score is calculated by looking at the number of payments over thirty days late, collections, judgements, and bankruptcies. This shows the likelihood of the person making their payments on time and whether it is risky to lend money them.

- **Current debts.** About 30 per cent of a FICO score considers how much the person currently owes. This indicates whether they're overextended on credit or not, and what the risk of defaulting on their payments is.

- **Length of credit history.** About 15 per cent of the score is based on how long the accounts have been open and how long it has been since each has been accessed. The longer an account has been open, the better from a credit score perspective, but having a long credit history isn't a prerequisite for a good FICO score.

- **Type of credit.** About 10 per cent of a FICO score is based on the mix of different types of credit the person has. These include bank loans, credit cards, revolving accounts, mortgages, and retail accounts.

- **New credit.** About 10 per cent of the score is based on how many new credit inquiries the account owner made in the last twelve months. The more credit accounts a person has applied for in a short period of time, the higher the risk of lending to them.

How Does VantageScore Work?

Like FICO, VantageScore uses a three-digit score to describe your credit history. Typically, a score of below 660 is considered riskier, while a healthy VantageScore is 661 and higher. The top score you can achieve with VantageScore is 850.

VantageScore 4.0—the most current model at the time of writing—uses a formula based on six factors. These are:

- **Payment history.** Payment history makes up 41 per cent of a person's VantageScore.
- **Depth of credit.** Twenty per cent of the Vantage-Score is based on the ages of all the different credit accounts, including the oldest, the newest, and the average age of the person's accounts, as well as whether they're revolving or instalment debts.
- **Credit utilization.** Another 20 per cent of the VantageScore looks at how much credit the individual has access to and how much of that they actually use each month.
- **Recent credit.** The number of recent hard credit inquiries made and new credit accounts opened makes up 11 per cent of a VantageScore.
- **Balances.** The total amount of money that is currently owed, including delinquent accounts, makes up 6 per cent of a VantageScore.
- **Available credit.** The amount of credit currently available to the account holder makes up 2 per cent of a VantageScore.

Chapter 14:
Identity Verifications

When BMP was about to sign a contract with a new United States supplier of criminal record checks, before signing with us, the company wanted to have an in-person meeting. This was one way for them to validate that BMP was a legitimate business, that we were who we said we were, and for them to ensure that we had the required security systems in place to safeguard confidential information. It was good practice by the supplier to perform the proper due diligence on BMP, even if they used one of the oldest methods of verifying identity: meeting face to face.

When COVID-19 hit the world in 2020, remote hiring became more common. This caused several concerns and issues—particularly the difficulties and complexities of confirming that a person really was who they said they were.

ID verifications confirm the authenticity and validity of a person's identity based on the information and documents they provide. This is extremely important for several different reasons, including remote hiring, financial transactions, access control, and online account creation.

Our clients, who had trusted us for years to ensure they knew who they were hiring, started to ask questions. How could they confirm that the person they were onboarding really was authentic? In response to this need, we launched our identity verification service.

There are many methods and technologies used for ID verification. The most common check is to verify if the documents provided are legitimate and belong to the candidate. This includes checking identity documents such as passports, driver's licences, as well as identity cards. The process could involve sending documents electronically to validate their authenticity. The candidate then typically takes a photograph of themselves, and software will match the ID to the face.

Biometric verification has started to come into play more often and is becoming increasingly sophisticated. This method uses a person's unique physical traits to verify their identity. Common biometric methods include fingerprint scanning, facial recognition, iris scanning, as well as voice recognition.

Knowledge-based verifications rely on a person's knowledge of certain information, such as passwords, personal identification numbers—or PINs—and answers to security questions. It is typically generated from data compiled from credit history and public records. Examples of knowledge tested in the questions might include past addresses, vehicle ownership, schools attended, mortgage details, and credit card accounts. This does add an extra layer of security.

The reasons to use identity verifications will only continue to increase, and the methods used to do so will become more and more sophisticated as technology evolves. The specific method used for ID verification depends on the level of security required and the reason it is requested.

Case Study

A case that was still ongoing at the time of writing this book shows how a simple identity check could have exposed a web of lies, fraud, and endangering people's lives. A woman who had posed as a nurse in British Columbia pleaded guilty to eleven charges, including assault, because the patients she had injected with dangerous medications would not have consented had they known she wasn't qualified.

The woman got jobs at two hospitals in British Columbia by submitting a resume containing fake references. One of these hospitals checked her references by email and the woman controlled the various email addresses.

Her professional registration number checked out, though. Except for one thing: It wasn't hers. She had stolen the identity of a real nurse who, after the case came to light, had to change

---

her surname in order to try and save her professional reputation.

Had the employers verified the fraudster's identity, they may have been alerted to do a criminal background check too. This would have revealed that the woman had a history of pretending to be a nurse, with accusations or convictions in Colorado as well as Ontario, Alberta, and British Columbia. Her parole following five years in prison in Alberta had expired only months before, and she had already committed fraud by stealing checks from a dental practice where she briefly worked after moving to British Columbia. At the time of writing, she was serving a seven-year prison sentence in Ontario.

Chapter 15:
Additional Checks

Depending on factors such as the job, the company, the industry, the country where the job is located, and even the country you're hiring the person from, there are additional checks you may want to perform.

Global Sanctions Check

The purpose of a global sanctions check is to ensure that the person isn't on an international watchlist for having links to criminal activities like money laundering, corruption and bribery, and terrorism. It's recommended especially for candidates from or working in other countries, who will have access to large sums of money or sensitive financial information.

It also checks whether the candidate is or has close ties to a politically exposed person, or PEP—someone with a prominent public function, such as a government official, a politician, or senior management in a state-owned enterprise. The reason for this is that PEPs and those close to them are considered at higher risk for corruption because they are in a position of influence.

Global sanctions checks have been part of background checks conducted in the United States for years. However, the BMP team is seeing more Canadian clients ordering these checks as remote hiring becomes more popular.

A good-quality global sanctions check scours databases from around the world, including international government organizations and law-enforcement agencies such as the FBI and Interpol. As a starting point for doing global sanctions checks from Canada, you can consult the Consolidated Canadian Autonomous Sanctions List.

Driving Record Check

Driving record checks are important not only for employees with access to a company vehicle, but also for those who are is required to drive for their job, even when they use their own vehicle. By ordering this important check for your potential employee, it will ensure your drivers are in good standing. It verifies that they have a valid driver's licence for the class of vehicle they'll be driving as part of their job. It's also important to know if they have any traffic-related violations or convictions or if they have a track record of safe driving. In addition, this kind of check is useful to help verify their identity.

Employers need to periodically recheck their drivers' records to ensure they are in good standing. Failure to do so could be interpreted as negligence on the part of the employer if a driver's conduct during their work ever leads to a court case.

The BMP team has a client in Canada who employs a number of drivers. Every time they hire a new employee, processing a driver abstract for that person is mandatory. However, the company goes one step further to ensure all their drivers are in good standing by having BMP run a new driver abstract every six months, on every single driver. One semi-annual check revealed that one of the drivers had lost their licence due to an impaired driving charge. The employee was terminated immediately. Our client informed us that if the employee had been honest, they would have found him an alternate employment opportunity within the company until his licence was reinstated.

In Canada, a driver's abstract can be ordered with consent from the candidate, on a province-by-province basis. A driver's abstract is the documented proof of all the person's driving records. It includes merit and demerit points, as well as any convictions and suspensions. The process to order a driver's abstract, as well as the turnaround time once you've ordered it, depends on the province or territory you require the check from. If you need a driver's abstract from Alberta, however, you need to ask the candidate to obtain a driver's abstract themselves, since this province doesn't allow third parties to order driver's abstracts. You'll then need to have a process in place to verify the authenticity of the document the candidate provides, since documents can be easily forged.

In the United States, the driving record will include the status of licence, driving points, citations, convictions, and traffic accidents. A third party wanting to obtain a copy of a person's driving record will require consent from that individual. An individual can also order one themselves by visiting their local Department of Motor Vehicles (DMV) or state driver's licensing office. There is a usually a fee involved, depending on the person's residential state.

Internationally, you will be required to verify a driver is properly licensed on a country-by-country basis. Many countries require a valid driver's licence along with an International Driving Permit, or IDP, which is typically valid for one year.

Immunizations

BMP has always conducted a great deal of work in the pharmaceutical space. In 1974, our first year in business, we onboarded our first pharmaceutical client. Over the decades, the pharmaceutical industry has become a niche market for us.

In July of 2013, a pharmaceutical client asked if we could track the immunization of their employees. The entrepreneur in me said yes, without any hesitation. I saw the look of concern in the face of my colleague, who was sitting across the table from me. I knew exactly what she was thinking: *How on earth are you going to do that?* But I've always had a hard time saying no to a client when they come to me with a problem to solve. And honestly, this is how great ideas are born.

The company wanted to ensure their healthcare workers, who are often visiting people's homes, are fully vaccinated. We added this service offering to our online order system so that the client could easily keep up to date on employee immunization. We determined that the client wanted to check that each of their employees had been immunized against the following diseases:

- Hepatitis B
- Measles, mumps, and rubella
- Varicella, or chicken pox
- Influenza
- Tuberculosis, or TB
- Tetanus, diphtheria, and pertussis
- COVID-19

In 2020, several of our clients wanted to be able track their employees' immunizations, especially once they started to return to the workplace in December 2021. Our immunization tracking program really took off at that time. Our marketing efforts, and my inability to say no to a client, were beneficial to us as a company. But more importantly, we provided a great service in addition to other strategies for companies to success-fully reopen their offices. This has truly proven to be a useful product to help ensure safe work environments.

When you order a check of a candidate's or employee's immunization records, it's important to always get the person's consent first and adhere to privacy laws that cover their medical information, such as PIPEDA in Canada, the *Health Insurance Portability and Accounting Act*, or HIPAA, in the United States, the GDPR in the European Union, and the *Data Protection Act* in the United Kingdom.

Chapter 16:
Exit and Stay Interviews

While not part of the authenticity verification of potential employees during the pre-hiring stage, utilizing exit and stay interviews (stay interviews are sometimes called retention interviews) can vastly improve company culture. Having a broader perspective of what is and isn't working for your employees will alert you to problems before they are too big to tackle, and it will help you strengthen everyday interactions. It will help you ensure you're a company where people want to work—and continue to work. Employees who feel aligned with your company's culture will perform better.

Exit and stay interviews were not common in the 1970s, at least not on a formal basis. They started to gain traction in the 1980s and became more commonplace in the 1990s. Both are very important for a company to implement into their hiring and employee retention programs. They offer valuable information as employees leave the organization, as well as throughout employment.

When we started with our investigative roots in 1974, there were no legal requirements about what could and could not be done in terms of speaking with employers about the performance of an employee, past or present.

In 2016, one of the leading banks in Canada came to BMP to ask for assistance with an exit interview program for their employees. This institution was aware of our reputation for being the leader in the executive reference-checking space and felt we could assist them. We jumped right in, developing a customized exit interview program that still exists today. This exit interview program has evolved and been tweaked many times over the years and still provides valuable information and insight to the bank as to the reasons employees leave.

It is best for companies to assign this important job to a third party. A person will be more inclined to open up to a third party instead of the actual employer, and they are more likely to do that in person rather than in response to an email or questionnaire. If done properly, a third party can help create an environment that is safe for the employee to share open and honest feedback, which the employer can use to foster a better work environment.

Exit Interviews

An exit interview is a survey-type conversation conducted when an employee is in the process of leaving a company. The main objective is to gather as much information as possible from the departing employees about their experiences, the reason for leaving if it is voluntary, and suggestions for how the company could improve. These suggestions for improvement are one of the most important pieces of information to obtain.

The timing of the interview is also very important. It's often done during the employee's final days or weeks at the company. If it's not conducted before the employee leaves, it lessens the opportunity to gather this valuable information, since the employee might be less inclined to speak to you once they've moved on.

Areas you may want to probe depend on whether it is a voluntary departure or a termination. However, in both situations, it's good practice to inquire about the workplace culture. Sometimes, this can open a can of worms, but it nearly always provides valuable feedback. It's also important to inquire about job satisfaction, how they felt about the management team, and areas for improvement or development.

Like in the reference-checking process, we stress the importance of always asking open-ended questions. You don't want the responses to be a yes or no. Ask what the person liked most about the job, what they disliked, why they decided to look for alternate employment, and what suggestions they have for the company to improve their employee retention. You want to foster more in-depth conversation to allow for seeing any holes in the information.

For several reasons, some employees may hesitate to provide honest feedback. Perhaps they fear retribution, or they don't want to leave on a negative note. This is important if they want to use that company as a reference. For that reason alone, it's important to create a safe and confidential environment. It is helpful to create an exit interview program for your company that is outsourced to a third party, like BMP. That way, the company will obtain more valuable and objective information and help to better understand why someone is leaving. After all, the purpose of an exit interview is to assess the overall employee experience within your organization and identify opportunities to improve retention and engagement.

Having a clear set of standards in place when conducting exit interviews can also play an essential role in risk management. Your job is to encourage dialogue. Ensure that the questions are relevant, respectful, and actionable. The exit interview is when an employee is most likely to reveal what they really think about the workload, issues with company culture, their real reasons for leaving, and other important questions you may have. You also want to ask what led them to begin searching for another opportunity. Depending on how they respond, that could help determine workplace concerns. Ask if they obtained the support needed to be successful. What did they like best and least about their job? Would they work for the company again? If not, ask why.

The information you obtain could then be used to develop or adjust an employee retention program. It can help in reducing employee turnover and increase overall productivity.

Depending on how soon before the employee's last day the exit interview is conducted, it may also be a good time for the employer to gather materials or company property, such as company phones and laptops, from the exiting employee.

Properly executed exit interviews will leave employees and employers with a sense of closure. Of course, there is no promise that they will end positively, but by attempting to be open to the feedback, the employer can create a safer work environment—one where people like to be. If employees feel valued, they will stay with you longer.

With one exit interview the BMP team conducted for a client, the employee was leaving of their own accord, and the employer had no idea that there were any issues. During the exit interview process, several issues were vocalized. We were able to determine the real reason the employee was leaving. Once the employer learned of the employee's concern and their reason for leaving, they were able to resolve their differences, and the employee ended up staying. This made us realize not only the value of conducting an exit interview, but also the importance of conducting retention interviews on an annual and sometimes a semi-annual basis.

Stay Interviews

Stay interviews are conducted like exit interviews, except they are conversations with current employees who aren't planning to leave—or at least haven't announced their intentions to leave yet. They are more preventive in nature.

The primary goal of a stay interview is for a company to understand an employee's job satisfaction. It's important to know how an employee feels about the company, their work, and how they're being supported. We all know the cost of replacing an employee—stay interviews can help a company become aware of issues in time to resolve them and increase their retention rates of all their valuable employees.

A good length for a stay interview is thirty minutes. However, the person conducting the interview should always allow more time in their calendar, in case the employee requires it. There could be concerns that arise during the interview process that the employee needs to have addressed at that moment. It would not be beneficial to have to cut them off in the middle of an important conversation. It's also important that the person conducting the interview schedules the proper time into their calendar to capture their notes and key takeaways after the interview.

Some companies will make stay interviews an annual occurrence. When sending a calendar invite to an employee, it's important to let them know the purpose and that it is not a regular weekly or monthly meeting. This will give everyone time to prepare properly so the meeting is more productive.

The one drawback, especially with large companies that have hundreds of employees, is the investment of time and the necessary resources to effectively conduct regular stay interviews and then to process, analyze, and incorporate the feedback. This is when weighing the risk versus benefit comes into play. Building a safe and effective work environment will pay off in the long run, and stay interviews help with that goal.

Conducting stay interviews is a great way to connect with existing employees to show them you care about their experience and their ideas and to proactively address any concerns they may have. Ideally, you will be able to identify pain points before they become full-blown problems. Stay interviews will not always lead to perfect outcomes, but if done properly, they will certainly lead to improved employee engagement.

Employee Surveys

Employee surveys are like retention interviews but tend to be less personalized and often more informal. They, too, are meant to gather information on employment engagement and overall satisfaction with their current work environment as well as with the management team.

There are many benefits to conducting employee surveys, including increased employee satisfaction, improved employee well-being, improved employee retention, more trust, and more empathy. Asking what your employees like the most and what they like the least will provide valuable insight. If you know what is not working, you then have time to fix it before things blow up.

Section 4:
Social Media

Chapter 17:
Social Media Checks

I'm thankful for the time in which I grew up. The stupid things people did in the 1960s was typically not made public, unless of course, worst-case scenario, they made the news. Nowadays, we share our entire lives on social media. We share our joys and frustrations. We celebrate our own and our loved ones' accomplishments and mourn our losses. And we use social media in our work lives too: to find a new job or recruit new employees, to share professional insights about the industry we work in, and to keep our employees and colleagues in the loop about company business.

This blending of our personal and professional lives online does present some issues, though. With what we're doing in our personal lives being put out there for everyone to see, we also give potential employers and clients a glimpse into who we are and the values we believe in. If our values clash with theirs, it can lead to problems—for us and for them.

Consumers hold companies to high values. What are companies doing to address social media? If you see poor conduct of your employees' online activity, why aren't you paying attention? What are you doing to address inappropriate online behaviour outside of your handbook policy? Are you being proactive? What about violence and safety?

The integration of social media into background checks and recruitment was slow to come into play. Many companies still tread carefully in this regard. However, as social media has become an important part of the lives of so many people, companies want to include social media checks. They want to know if they can get a glimpse into who the potential candidate really is—or at least what they tell the world about who they are.

The Rabbit Hole

Hiring someone without being sure how they present themselves on social media has become a business risk. But does your HR team have the time and are they being paid to scroll through someone's Facebook feed and scan through every post, including all the detours that may come with it? It's a rabbit hole to be avoided at all costs. Even if an employee has the time, it can get messy playing detective. What do they look for? And have they created a program that is fair and consistent for everyone?

As we noted before, once you see something, you can't unsee it. Just by exposing yourself to online information, you're more likely to be unfair in your decision-making process. When you pull up a person's social media profile, the moment you open the page, there is a wide range of protected class information that jumps out: their national origin or ancestry, their sex, marital status, gender identity, physical or mental disabilities, even their age.

I'm certain these are areas that everyone is aware of. They definitely should not be used in the hiring process. Viewing protected class information can open some liability risks for companies by creating biases, whether intentional or not. This is all information that we can redact out of our report.

Social media platforms use several sophisticated algorithms that are meant to keep a user engaged by showing them content that they are more likely to interact with. This is where valuable time can be lost, because the incredible amount of content on social media platforms makes it difficult to stop scrolling. It can be very addictive. We keep scrolling because every click or swipe means we could discover something new, and that allows the dopamine to keep coming.

Of course, with the vast amount of information and content available on social media platforms, there *is* always something new to see. And to make it even more difficult to resist, social media algorithms customize content to match users' preferences and interests.

The team at BMP aims to help our clients avoid the social media rabbit hole, and we act as a third party for many to investigate a potential new employee's social media activities, as well as to examine current employees' activities. Initially, BMP conducted our own social media checks in-house, manually combing through the platforms. Then in 2014, while I was attending the PBSA annual conference in Denver, Colorado, I met a lady in line during the cocktail hour. We started chatting and it turned out she had a company that conducted social media checks for employers. This was becoming a more and more important part of the hiring process. I quickly learned the importance of outsourcing our social media checks to a third party who already had the advanced technology to complete the checks thoroughly and in a timely manner, rather than manually. BMP partnered with this company and soon noticed how much more efficient the process was. More importantly, by using technology specifically designed to access the information our clients needed, reports were more thorough and comprehensive. We were able to obtain information that would have taken hours to search in the past. Having customized software to process our social media reduced the turnaround and provided more content in a fraction of the time. Most importantly, our team avoided the social media rabbit hole.

Conducting a Social Media Check

The proliferating use of social media has led to concerns about privacy and legal considerations—something to be mindful of. What may have been acceptable at some point, may no longer be today. So, we caution employers to be mindful of the amount of digging they do online and to ensure it is only public information that they report on.

When the BMP team is ordering a social media check for one of our clients, we must obtain written consent from the candidate before we initiate the process. We require a copy of the candidate's most recent resume and identification. This information is then entered into our social media order centre. The more information that we enter, the more information we get back in the social media report.

Information that is required to order the social media check includes:

- Current resume, including current and past employers and dates of employment; education information
- Full legal name and any former name
- Email address
- Mailing address
- Phone number
- Date of birth
- All social media profile handles

Once this information is entered into our platform, a social media background report is generated. The report is broken down into the posts the candidate engaged with and whether they authored a post or simply commented, or just liked it.

A social media background report involves a combination of technology and human analytics. It's important to have access to the proper technology to assist in this important task and avoid going down the rabbit hole; however, the human analytic aspect is crucial because you must be certain that you have researched the correct John Doe in your online search. Once a candidate's profile is identified by the BMP team, the content is reviewed, and the report generated.

For social media reports processed in the United States, any federally or state-protected class information must be redacted. In Canada, our reports adhere to two federal privacy laws that are enforced by the Office of the Privacy Commissioner of Canada. They are the *Privacy Act*, which covers how the federal government handles personal information, and PIPEDA, which covers how businesses handle personal information.

The social media reports generated by the BMP team provide valuable insights into a candidate's online behaviour and appropriateness as someone who is a fit for the company's basic code of conduct, values, or social media policy, and limit the risk of a negligent hire. All information provided in the reports can be actionable towards a hiring decision. For employment purposes, our searches typically go back seven years, but sometimes it might be necessary to go back even further.

Case Study

The moment you post something on the internet, it is there forever, and your social media posts can come back to haunt you and hurt your career many years later. When the professional soccer club CF Montréal hired a new professional coach in January 2023, I'm certain they didn't expect or want to be looking for a replacement within twenty-four hours. But that's what happened after an old social media

---

post surfaced that made it impossible to keep the coach in the role.

In response to an incident during a victory speech being delivered by Parti Québécois leader Pauline Marois in 2012, where a gunman opened fire, killing one person and injuring another, Sandro Grande allegedly posted something suggesting that the only mistake the shooter made was to miss his target.

His Twitter comments resurfaced when he got the job with the Montreal soccer club just over a decade later, and politicians from four different Quebec political parties as well as Montreal's mayor condemned his appointment. Grande initially insisted that someone hacked his social media account and denied ownership of the post, but his contract with the professional sports club, where the coach must be a role model for the team and in the community, was cancelled nevertheless. He later admitted that he had been responsible for the posts after all.

What To Look For

A major concern, and maybe the number one reason larger organizations reach out to us, is the risk of bad publicity. Nobody needs an employee's crazy Facebook post hitting the news. You know the saying: No news is good news. An employee's negative or derogatory post is one of the worst types of news a company can receive. There is a duty of care that consumers and the general public expect companies to take in today's world. Efficiently screening candidates' or employees' social media is one of them.

So what social media content is impactful to employment? The BMP team looks specifically for any workplace safety issues such as racism or intolerance, violence, and potential illegal activity, like the sharing of sexually explicit material. If one of your clients can easily pull up a quick Google search on a member of your team or an employee and find adverse content, they are likely asking why the company did not do the same thing. They'll want to know why you hired this employee and why you are not doing something about this content.

Also, outside of external risks, social media can cause internal problems within a company. An employee or a group of employees may view someone making a racist post on Facebook, for example, as the equivalent of them standing up in the office and yelling the same thing. What we commonly hear about this type of issue is that it started in the workplace and ended up online, or that it started online and ended up in the workplace. Once this happens, you now have a major problem to deal with.

Case Study

While we typically focus on the candidate's own social media, it is important for employees to remember that their conduct in public can have severe consequences for them when it ends up on someone else's social media. With most people now using cellphones with built-in video cameras, there are many cases of people's behaviour, both on and off the clock, being filmed and going viral. There are entire social media channels dedicated to so-called "Karen" videos.

One case of note not only had severe consequences for the people directly involved, but also sparked a global movement.

In May 2020, four police officers in Minneapolis were filmed by a teenaged girl as they arrested George Floyd. While Floyd was lying face down in the street with his hands cuffed behind his back, one of the officers, Derek Chauvin, used his knee to press down on Floyd's neck. Two other officers, Thomas Lane and J. Alexander Kueng, held Floyd down, while the fourth officer, Tou Thao, held onlookers at bay, preventing them from helping Floyd. More than nine minutes later, Floyd died, having been unable to breathe.

The video was released on social media and immediately went viral, so the Minneapolis Police Department fired all four officers by the next day. They were later charged, found guilty, and sent to prison for the parts they played in Floyd's death, with Chauvin having to serve the longest sentence: twenty-two years and six months.

Even though the Minneapolis Police Department acted quickly in firing the officers when the video went viral, they paid a heavy price too. They came under federal review by the United States Department of Justice, which found serious problems within the culture of the department and seriously damaged their reputation. The Minneapolis City Council suffered too: in 2021, they reached a settlement in a civil lawsuit filed against them by Floyd's family, having to pay twenty-seven million dollars.

The case also sparked protests around the world to raise awareness of police brutality and racism. While most of these protests were peaceful, some—including in the Minneapolis–Saint Paul area—turned violent, with thousands of other businesses suffering damage due to vandalism and looting.

There are other areas of concern for businesses too. For example, HR is picking up on a lot of buzzwords used across social media—terms like "quiet quitting" and "ghost jobs." Employees are using social media to discuss their workplace situations. Employers want to know who is saying what.

A company does not want to hire someone who is complaining about something, especially when it's chronic. It's not healthy to have negative people in your workforce. Also, we keep an eye out for strong opinions, rants of any type, as well as posting overly personal photos.

During the COVID-19 outbreak, there were many differences of opinion on how to best manage the pandemic. Social media contributed a great deal of misinformation about COVID-19 and accepting the vaccine, and it created conflict in the workplace. Employers were seeing information from their employees online that they were not comfortable with. It then became a problem that had to be dealt with. In some cases, it resulted in people leaving of their own accord or companies terminating their employment based on social media posts.

In summary, there are many ways social media activity can be impactful to employment. As an employer, take the time required to be aware of what a potential employee is putting out for the world to see before bringing them on board.

Outsourcing this important task to an objective third party helps to protect companies from the bad decisions employees have made in the past. We are only capable and legally allowed to view publicly available information and because of that, these reports are also a litmus test of sorts, testing an individual's level of responsibility. If someone is the type of person to behave poorly online and has it all out there for the public to see, can that person be trusted to represent your company appropriately?

But conducting a comprehensive pre-employment screening check on a potential candidate takes time. We had a case where our client ordered the social media search as an afterthought. They asked us to rush the check. We began the process right away and immediately found derogatory information on the potential candidate. The client reached out to the candidate for clarification. Once it was confirmed that it was indeed the correct person, the client did not move forward with the candidate. They had to begin the expensive process of starting to look for a new candidate all over again. However, if they had made a poor hiring decision and brought the wrong person on board, it would have cost a lot more down the road to go through the entire process again.

Chapter 18:
Social Media Policies

It's strongly encouraged that a company has a social media policy for all their employees and ensures that attention is brought to it during the hiring process.

Companies also need to be mindful of the actual time their employees spend on social media during business hours and how it can affect their productivity. We've found this more problematic since COVID-19 hit in 2020 and more companies started hiring employees to work remotely. It became increasingly difficult to know how much time employees were spending on social media. It's important for companies to implement a social media monitoring process and for being clear about it in the written social media policy. This could safeguard your company against any legal issues if you have to terminate an employee because of excessive social media use.

There are many products available today to assist with this. However, what is most crucial is to educate your employees as to why this is important, why these policies are in place, and the consequences of violating them, and then to enforce this policy. The successful implementation of a social media policy within a company takes time but, if done properly, can save an employer a great deal of money as well as lost productivity.

Dealing with Unsavory Posts

So, what happens when one of your employees has posted negative or derogatory content to a social media platform and it goes viral?

A company reached out to BMP when they learned that an employee had made a racist comment online. It was affecting the workplace, with a reduction in employee morale and interpersonal relations in the office. The company was unsure how to react to this racist post. BMP advised the company to address the issue with the employee right away and try to understand the reasoning for the post. It appeared the employee did not understand the ramifications of that post, and they apologized. The company asked the employee to remove the post, and they willingly did. It also sent a strong message to the other employees about what was acceptable, and what was not, in terms of their social media conduct.

The situation ended well for the company and the employee. However, once the company realized what could have happened, they implemented a social media policy. They brought in an outside firm to help set the stage and had training sessions for the employees. Everyone was made aware of their boundaries, and the workplace environment improved. The open line of communication was critical. As a result, this company asked us to conduct social media checks on all of their employees on an annual basis.

We are seeing more companies implementing social media policies for their employees, even when they are not officially representing the company. Still, chances are high that at some point, a company will have an employee who will post something that is not appropriate and could reflect poorly on the brand of the company. It may not be intentional at all, but it happens often. To assist in mitigating the damage and to avoid negative content being posted, it's important that the employer keeps the situation from blowing up. It seems that weekly, there is some sort of news report on what should be a private or an embarrassing event going public. What happens when it is one of your employees?

Every company today should discuss their employee social media policy at the onboarding stage. Employees must understand that companies will act to address off-duty conduct that could affect the company brand. If people are not aware of the importance of their online presence when they are first hired, it may be difficult to call them out on a post that may not be appropriate later in their employment. The law regarding an employer's response to off-duty employment conduct has evolved over time as employers and employees are more and more tied together outside of regular business hours. The job of the HR team has become more complex as a result. It has become a learning curve for many companies on how to manage negative or derogatory posts from employees.

When an employee's negative social media post goes viral, the company must deal with the situation as quickly as possible. One of the most important concerns is reputation damage to the company. Companies that are reputable and have a long-standing history of being a great place to work, can quickly have their reputation damaged by a disgruntled employee or customer.

If a controversial post goes live, the first step is to have a conversation with the employee as to why they posted the content and ensure they understand the ramifications of posting that specific content. A person may have posted something and was not aware of the potential damage to their employer. To start the reputation control process for your company, explain to the employee why this is an issue for your company, and recommend that the individual who is responsible for the posted content takes it down. Depending on the extent of the damage and the size of the company, you may consider bringing in a public relations management team to help resolve the issue so that employees feel comfortable and supported, and to quickly reinstate the reputation of the company.

There could also be legal ramifications. These could include breach of confidentiality and the violation of privacy, that could potentially lead to legal action against the company. If it's confirmed that the post violates the company's code of conduct, a company may choose to terminate employment, even if the post was done outside of business hours or on personal accounts. Finding the right way to deal with an employee's social media posts can become a nightmare for an employer when they're not objective about the content of the offending posts and appear to be taking sides.

Case Study

Three days after the October 7, 2023 terror attacks on Israel by Hamas militants, a nephrologist in Ontario who had a decade's worth of experience volunteering as a doctor in Gaza, replied to a post on X to debunk some misinformation it was spreading. This led to accusations of antisemitism and denying the Holocaust—some of these levelled by colleagues at the hospital where the doctor worked—as well as his home address being made public and threats made, including one called in to the hospital. Within twenty-four hours, the hospital suspended the doctor for a month.

The decision by the hospital to act so swiftly against this doctor but not against the other colleagues involved caused internal tension among employees, as well as bad publicity for them in the media. It also led to a lawsuit against them by the doctor.

As difficult as an inappropriate social media post from an employee is, one from a customer can be even more serious and damaging to your brand. All companies should strive to provide world-class customer service. One of the reasons BMP is celebrating fifty years in business in 2024 is because of our world-class customer service. When there is an issue with customer service, the company's job is to fix it, immediately. And always apologize like you mean it. Own it. You don't want any negative social media posts from a customer going viral.

Case Study

In 2008, Dave Carroll witnessed United Airlines baggage handlers in Chicago throwing his band's musical instruments during their stopover on a flight from Halifax, Nova Scotia to Omaha, Nebraska. Carroll's expensive, custom-made guitar was broken, despite having been packed securely in a padded case. He sought compensation from the airline, but after nine months of having been given the runaround and then told to stop calling, the Canadian musician decided to do what he does best—he wrote a trilogy of songs about it.

As soon as he uploaded the first song to YouTube, it went viral and caused a public relations disaster for the airline. While they pledged to make it right and change the culture of their customer service, the "United Breaks Guitars" trilogy still haunts them to this day and the case has been the subject of numerous academic theses and articles on what *not* to do when handling customer complaints in the age of social media.

If negative information gets to the media, you now have a much bigger problem to deal with. What is most important is that you respond to the issue as a unified team. Ensure you take the time to thoroughly address the issue and gather all pertinent facts. Then you need to take ownership of the problem and fix it.

This also means being transparent. Explain what happened, and what solutions you have put in place to ensure it does not happen again. Always be accountable.

You'll need to work hard to build back the trust of your client and restore your brand reputation. This can be done, in most cases, and it will be worth the time and effort that it will take to make things right.

Learn from it. Put in place processes and improvements so that it never happens again.

Chapter 19:
Social Media Recruiting

Social media and hiring are connected in so many ways. Social media recruiting involves using a variety of social media platforms, such as LinkedIn, Facebook, X, and Instagram, to source out potential candidates when trying to fill a role within a company.

The team at BMP finds the most popular platform used today for job-related content is LinkedIn, which has been a subsidiary of Microsoft since December 2016. LinkedIn is predominantly used to find employment, to find potential candidates for employment purposes, and to strengthen professional networks. However, members also use LinkedIn to stay updated on industry news and to share and learn new skills.

As part of the BMP Know Your Customer Program, we use LinkedIn as one method in determining whether a company we are bringing on as a new client is a legitimate business.

If used properly, social media can assist in the important task of finding great employees. A company's social media platform can assist in reaching a wider pool of job candidates, as well as a diverse range of candidates. Promoting your company helps to attract great talent. It's also a great way to showcase the company culture and to build relationships with customers, prospects, and other businesses.

Recruiters and HR professionals are increasingly using social networking as a hiring tool. There can be many benefits, including learning more about the potential candidate as a person, how they conduct themselves in public—which you can also glean from any comments, both negative and positive, about their professional history—and, once you understand their demeanor, determining if that person might be a good fit for the company. As explained in the previous chapter, this can assist in protecting your company image. If you hire someone who has a negative social media presence, that could affect the overall culture of the company.

The team at BMP has always preferred hiring on a referral basis when possible. One of the advantages of this is the reduction of the actual screening time when bringing on a new employee. It also helps to encourage employee engagement, retention, and satisfaction. And then there is also the potential savings in terms of recruitment fees. Several companies offer a referral fee to the employee who successfully makes a recommendation; however, it will typically be lower than what they would have to pay to a recruitment firm. If you are using a referral system, it's important to be aware of the longevity of the existing employee and their reputation within the organization.

As with any process, there are disadvantages. But when looking at an employee referral program, the disadvantages do not outweigh the advantages. One of the disadvantages is that the recommendation will be biased. Most of the time, an employee could make a legitimate referral; however, at times it could be more self-serving to the employee making the referral. It could also encourage negative company energy that could affect the dynamics of the company employee base. One of the worst-case scenarios is if one of the employees decides to leave. Is the company at risk of losing both employees? The retention of good employees is critical to the success of your company.

There is a wide range of statistics regarding social media recruiting, depending on the platform that you look at. However, it's safe to say that almost half of all Millennial and Gen Z workers have applied for jobs they have found through social media. In addition, a majority of employers are using social networks to locate new talent. And very few hiring managers would consider hiring a candidate without looking at their online presence.

Social media recruiting takes time and work to get right. However, if done properly, it can help in making a great hire for a low-cost recruiting effort.

Section 5:
In Conclusion

Chapter 20:
Making an Informed
Hiring Decision

If you've been with me from the beginning of the book, you'll likely know a few concepts I have emphasized more than once. But, if you were to end up forgetting everything else, there is just one saying that is at the heart of everything I've shared, that will help you remember everything else: hire slowly, fire quickly!

There's a good reason why I've repeated this phrase several times. It illustrates the risk involved in approaching the hiring process in a rush. Take the annual salary of the role you're hiring for, multiply it by between one and three, and that's the full estimated cost of how much it will take to replace the employee if you don't get it right on the first try. Pretty expensive, isn't it?

This book has been about making absolutely sure your focus is on all the right places, and you make the right call the first time.

When hiring, you're in one of the most important seats in your company. Any decisions you make will have traceable effects throughout the organization. You're not only making sure that a candidate is a good mix of great qualifications for the job and culture fit for the company but are also ensuring that the information you are using to make these decisions has not been gamed in any way.

If the information you're depending on to choose one candidate over another isn't true, then it won't matter if every other process during hiring is perfect, because you don't know your candidate at all. This is referred to as negligent hiring because it is indeed an oversight to invest that much trust in an individual and to hang your company's goals on the frail thread of their word. People lie, and job candidates are just that—people!

Throughout the book, I've also done a breakdown of the different types of checks that can be conducted, to explain why each one is important, so that you know which will be most beneficial for you. To recap:

- Reference checks are to ensure that the references the candidate listed on their resume are indeed who they say they are. They are helpful for determining how truthful the candidate has been in the way they're representing themselves in their application and can give you information about the candidate's personality and work ethic that you wouldn't have had otherwise.

- Employment verifications are to check that the candidate is truthful about their job title and dates of employment. They will alert you to a candidate's attempts to hide gaps in employment and to misrepresent their actual skills and experience.

- Education verifications are to check that the candidate is truthful about the academic qualifications and certifications needed for the job. They also verify that any professional accreditations are up to date.

- Criminal record checks ensure that there isn't anything in the candidate's past that can put the company, its other employees, and its clients at risk.

- Credit checks look at the job applicant's financial situation and credit history. These checks are mainly recommended for candidates who will have access to large sums of money, to reduce the risk of financial mismanagement and fraud.

- Identity verifications are to check that the candidate is who they say they are. These checks have become increasingly important with the rise of remote hiring, where you may never meet the candidate in person.

- Global sanctions checks are to alert you to candidates who may be involved in, or close to someone who is involved in crimes such as money laundering, corruption, and political violence across borders.

- Driving record checks ensure that anybody who will be driving as part of their job duties or have access to company vehicles has an up-to-date and relevant driver's licence, without any traffic violations.

- Immunization checks are to verify that the candidate has been immunized against diseases they may be at higher risk of contracting or spreading during the course of their work. This is especially important for candidates who work in healthcare, the pharmaceutical industry, and with animals.
- Social media checks help reduce the risk of damage to the company's reputation and employee morale due to adverse social media content.

I want to reiterate that you don't need to conduct *all* these checks on *all* of the candidates for *all* of the jobs you're recruiting for. You need to decide what's best for your business, and act accordingly. However, I recommend that you enlist the help of background-screening experts rather than do everything yourself. They can also help you with exit and retention interviews. They will save you time and money, are well versed in the legal framework within which you can conduct background checks and, perhaps most importantly, they remain neutral.

Now, I want to put it back to you. Think of a time when you made a bad hire and what you could have done differently. Now that you understand the complexities of the process and how important it is to know who you are hiring, what are you going to do differently when you make the next hire? And going forward, what will you add to your pre-employment screening process before making that important decision to ensure you really know who you are hiring?

Some Final Thoughts

It has been exciting to witness the transformation and evolution of the industry and the screening practices over the last five decades.

Finishing this book that sought to distill industry insights for hiring professionals is the best fiftieth-anniversary gift I could think of for BMP, for my father who started BMP fifty years ago, and the people that have loved it over the years—or decades! It has all been a long time coming. We've poured so much into what we do.

With the advancement of technology including artificial intelligence and innovation, I'm excited to see how the industry will continue to evolve in the years to come. Current issues covered in the media, in Canada and elsewhere around the world, show us that the background checking industry and verifications related to hiring and employment are continuing to evolve.

There are some areas I'll be watching, especially with respect to identity verification. For instance, false claims of indigenous ancestry have recently been making headlines in Canada and the United States, with some involving high-profile figures like Buffy Sainte-Marie, Sacheen Littlefeather, and Elizabeth Warren. Indigenous people may have access to special social and education programs and can enjoy other benefits, including tax related, not accessible to those who aren't members of an Indigenous nation or tribe. Where there are diversity, equity and inclusion—or DEI—programs or affirmative action laws in place in order to redress the effects of unfair discrimination in the past, a candidate's ancestry is a factor in their chances of getting the job.

Also, governments in Canada, the US, and Australia and New Zealand are looking to procurement policies to help ensure a portion of public sector contracts are awarded to indigenous businesses. This adds pressure on companies and the people who run them to find all possible avenues to make themselves eligible for these contracts, which may, in turn, lead to increased requirements for indigenous identity verification services.

But how would one go about verifying someone's ancestry without breaking privacy laws? And how do you prevent using methods to define someone's ancestry like those used for racial classification during South Africa's apartheid era, and breaking anti-discrimination laws? During apartheid, for example, fifty and sixty years ago the government in South Africa would issue documentation to parents after the birth of a child to notify them how the child was classified. Depending on whether they were classified as "white" or "black," for example, the baby had much of their future decided for them: where they could live, go to school, work, who they could marry, even which park benches they could sit on. And, of course, whether they could vote. There are also terrible stories of what happened to people who got "reclassified" and lost everything. We of course do not want to be going down that road in Canada.

There are also verification challenges related to other DEI categories—sexuality, race, religion, etcetera. What is the appropriate vehicle to verify that someone does, indeed, belong to one of these categories?

These are just some of the questions that I and my team are digging into at the time of writing. We've talked about circumstances where public-facing posts on social media have caused a stir, both for the employee and the employer. But what about so-called private communications? Just as we were putting the finishing touches on this book, Global News reported on the case of three RCMP officers from Coquitlam, BC who are the subjects of a police code of conduct investigation. The three officers are alleged to have posted racist, sexist, and homophobic messages on private group chats on WhatsApp, Signal, and internal RCMP mobile data terminals. The officers have been suspended pending the outcome of code of conduct hearings. In the Global News report, Arthur Schafer with the Centre for Applied Ethics said, "Where is the leadership of the force in setting hiring guidelines that will select people who can be appropriate?"

Straight-up identity verification alone conducted during the hiring process wouldn't likely reveal potentially problematic biases or attitudes that conflict with the values of the hiring organization and the communities being served. Social media checks may have, but not if the individuals were careful about what they posted. The question that arises for me when I think about the case above is, where do organizations draw the line between private and public conversations? How do hiring policies articulate requirements for the attitudes and beliefs their employees hold? Thankfully, I'm not the one who must find the answers to those questions. I'm just the one who will be able to help these organizations verify that the people they're looking to hire are who they say they are and have all the right requirements for the job.

Acknowledgements

The writing process has been enjoyable, thought provoking, challenging, emotional, and difficult at times. I'm honoured to have had the opportunity to reflect on how the background screening industry has evolved over the last fifty years, how world events have helped shape the industry, how we've had to adapt and pivot to ensure our beloved clients know who they are hiring.

Dad, I wish you could be here today to see what we've built together. I believe you would be proud. Your vision and hard work laid the foundation for everything we've achieved over the last fifty years. I've tried to honour your legacy while also making it my own. Thank you for the values you instilled in me and for always believing in this company. I wish you could see how far we've come.

Thank you to Anne Day and Marg Hachey, BAG (Book Accountability Group) ladies, WPO (Women's President Organization) and all my WPO sisters. My fellow WBEs (Women Business Enterprise) who have been a valuable support system to me over the years through WBE Canada and WEConnect International. Preston Conohan of policecheck.com and Michelle Leblond of the Professional Background Screening Association also provided valuable feedback on earlier drafts of this manuscript.

Thanks to publisher Boni Wagner-Stafford and the team at Ingenium Books. From the very beginning, their professionalism and expertise were evident. I did not have experience in writing a book and they guided me through the publishing process with clear communication and valuable insights.

What impressed me most was their attention to detail and ability to capture my voice while enhancing the manuscript. The editorial feedback was constructive and thorough, resulting in a polished final product that exceeded my expectations.

Thanks to their dedication, my book will reach a wider audience than I imagined. I wholeheartedly recommend Boni and her amazing supporting cast to anyone looking for a talented and supportive publishing team!

And thank you to all the amazing customers and clients of BMP—past, present, and future. My customers are the reason I get up every day.

One thing I hope will remain constant, long after I'm gone, is the importance of customer service. The customer is the reason you get up every day. You may not always like them, but you should always love them. Remember, the customer may not always be right, but it's your job to make them feel that they are.

Work hard at giving your beloved clients the wow factor in everything you do.

From the bottom of my heart, I'm wishing you great success in making brilliant hires. With the right people in the right seats, there is nothing you can't do. Most importantly, always continue to keep a human component in everything you do.

A company does not get to turn fifty years old without world-class customer service.

End of story.

About the Author

Marty and her team at Britton Management Profiles (BMP) have helped thousands of companies know who they are hiring over the last fifty years.

Marty left her civil engineering job in 1994 and took over BMP when her father, David G. Britton, became ill. At that time, it was an investigative and executive reference-checking business. Over the decades, Marty and her team have continued to expand their pre-employment screening services, making sure their clients hire solid candidates.

She's an active member of the Professional Background Screening Association (PBSA), where she has served on a number of PBSA boards, including as chair of the Canadian board in 2020. She is also a proud member of the Women's President Organization, a peer-to-peer advisory committee board. BMP is a certified member of both WBE Canada and WEConnect International.

Marty lives in Toronto with her husband Ed. She's proud of her two adult children, even more so than the company she has steered for three decades. She is an avid walker and enjoys spending time outside, especially on a golf course. She also enjoys spending time with family and friends at the cottage—their happy place—in Prince Edward County.

Bibliography

Baska, Maggie. "Pilot who listed Star Wars character as reference must repay training costs." People Management. CIPD. September 4, 2018. https://www.peoplemanagement. co.uk/article/1747035/pilot-listed-star-wars-character-reference-repay-training-costs

Basken, Paul. "Canadian Universities Tackle False Claims of Indigenous Identities." July 27, 2022. Inside Higher Ed. https://www.insidehighered.com/news/2022/07/28/canadian-universities-tackle-false-claims-indigenous-identities

Basu, Brishti. "Ontario doctor suspended, his address published after pro-Palestinian social media posts." CBC News. CBC/Radio-Canada. October 20, 2023. https://www.cbc.ca/news/canada/doctor-doxed-suspended-palestinian-posts-1.7001887

CBC News. "Broken guitar song gets airline's attention." CBC/Radio-Canada. July 8, 2009. https://www.cbc.ca/news/entertainment/broken-guitar-song-gets-airline-s-attention-1.802741

De Luce, Dan, Laura Strickler and Ari Sen. "Senior Trump official embellished résumé, had face on fake Time cover." NBC News. NBC Universal. November 12, 2019. https://www.nbcnews.com/politics/donald-trump/senior-trump-official-embellished-resume-had-face-fake-time-cover-n1080356

Dujay, John. "Montreal soccer coach fired after 1 day over social media comments." Canadian HR Reporter. January 12, 2023. https://www.hrreporter.com/focus-areas/recruitment-and-staffing/montreal-soccer-coach-fired-after-1-day-over-social-media-comments/372817

Federal Trade Commission. "Fair Credit Reporting Act." Accessed September 13, 2024. https://www.ftc.gov/legal-library/browse/statutes/fair-credit-reporting-act

Federal Trade Commission. "Gramm-Leach-Bliley Act." Accessed September 13, 2024. https://www.ftc.gov/legal-library/browse/statutes/gramm-leach-bliley-act

Ferrazzi, Keith. "Technology Can Save Onboarding from Itself." Harvard Business Review. March 25, 2015. https://hbr.org/2015/03/technology-can-save-onboarding-from-itself

Fonseca, Felicia. "Warren still dogged by past claims of indigenous ancestry." PBS News. NewsHour Productions LLC.

February 27, 2020. https://www.pbs.org/newshour/politics/
warren-still-dogged-by-past-claims-of-indigenous-ancestry

Gov.UK. "Data protection." Accessed September 13, 2024.
https://www.gov.uk/data-protection

Gov.UK. "Equality Act 2010: guidance." June 16, 2015.
https://www.gov.uk/guidance/equality-act-2010-guidance

Gov.UK. "Guidance on the Rehabilitation of Offenders Act
1974 and the Exceptions Order 1975." October 28, 2023.
https://www.gov.uk/government/publications/new-guidance-
on-the-rehabilitation-of-offenders-act-1974

Government of Canada. "Consolidated Canadian Autonomous
Sanctions List." August 14, 2024. https://www.international.
gc.ca/world-monde/international_relations-relations_interna-
tionales/sanctions/consolidated-consolide.aspx?lang=eng

Government of Canada. "What is a record suspension?"
October 19, 2018. https://www.canada.ca/en/parole-board/
services/record-suspensions/what-is-a-record-suspension.html

Hetler, Amanda. "59 trending HR buzzwords." TechTarget.
July 2, 2024. https://www.techtarget.com/whatis/feature/
Trending-HR-buzzwords

Internet Crime Complaint Center. "Deepfakes and Stolen PII
Utilized to Apply for Remote Work Positions." June 28, 2022.
https://www.ic3.gov/Media/Y2022/PSA220628

Jamieson, Alastair. "Musician behind anti-airline hit video
'United Breaks Guitars' pledges more songs." The Telegraph.

Telegraph Media Group Limited. July 23, 2009. https://www.telegraph.co.uk/travel/travelnews/5892082/Musician-behind-anti-airline-hit-video-United-Breaks-Guitars-pledges-more-songs.html

Keeler, Jacqueline. "Sacheen Littlefeather was a Native American icon. Her sisters say she was an ethnic fraud." San Francisco Chronicle. Hearst Communications, Inc. October 22, 2022. https://www.sfchronicle.com/opinion/openforum/article/Sacheen-Littlefeather-oscar-Native-pretendian-17520648.php

Lapierre, Matthew. "Montreal pro soccer coach, who was quickly fired for offensive tweets, apologizes." CBC News. CBC/Radio-Canada. January 19, 2023. https://www.cbc.ca/news/canada/montreal/sovereignists-quebec-grande-cf-montreal-1.6719431

Leo, Geoff, Roxanna Woloshyn and Linda Guerriero. "Who is the real Buffy Sainte-Marie?" CBC News. CBC/Radio-Canada. October 27, 2023. https://www.cbc.ca/newsinteractives/features/buffy-sainte-marie

Lindsay, Bethany. "Serial nurse impostor faces new assault and fraud charges in Victoria." CBC News. CBC/Radio-Canada. August 16, 2024. https://www.cbc.ca/news/canada/british-columbia/brigitte-cleroux-view-royal-charges-1.6937203

Morris, Kathy. "Survey: How Many People Lie on their Resumes?" Zippia, Inc. March 2, 2020. https://www.zippia.com/advice/how-many-people-lie-on-resumes-survey/

Murray, Conor. "U.S. Data Privacy Protection Laws: A Comprehensive Guide." Forbes. Forbes Media LLC. April 25, 2023. https://www.forbes.com/sites/conormurray/2023/04/21/us-data-privacy-protection-laws-a-comprehensive-guide/

MyFICO. "What is a FICO® Score?" FICO. Fair Isaac Corporation. Accessed September 13, 2024. https://www.myfico.com/credit-education/what-is-a-fico-score

Office of Privacy and Civil Liberties. "Privacy Act of 1974." U.S. Department of Justice. October 4, 2022. https://www.justice.gov/opcl/privacy-act-1974

Office of the Privacy Commissioner of Canada. "How PIPEDA applies to charitable and non-profit organizations." June 25, 2019. https://www.priv.gc.ca/en/privacy-topics/privacy-laws-in-canada/the-personal-information-protection-and-electronic-documents-act-pipeda/r_o_p/02_05_d_19/

Ontario. "Police record checks." January 15, 2024. https://www.ontario.ca/page/police-record-checks

Paradkar, Shree. "This doctor was suspended after his tweets on the Israel-Hamas conflict drew controversy. Now he's suing." Toronto Star. Toronto Star Newspapers Limited. March 24, 2024. https://www.thestar.com/news/this-doctor-was-suspended-after-his-tweets-on-the-israel-hamas-conflict-drew-controversy-now/article_3e35892c-e7cc-11ee-8e35-0b9799155c0a.html

Peopletrail. "History of Background Checks." October 19, 2023. https://peopletrail.com/history-of-background-checks/

Royal Canadian Mounted Police. "Criminal record checks." September 12, 2024. https://www.rcmp-grc.gc.ca/en/criminal-record-checks

Shapiro, Emily and Whitney Lloyd. "$27 million settlement for George Floyd's family approved by Minneapolis City Council." ABC News. March 12, 2021. https://abcnews.go.com/US/27-million-settlement-george-floyds-family-approved-minneapolis/story?id=76419755

The Associated Press. "Derek Chauvin, ex-officer convicted of murdering George Floyd, moved to new prison after being stabbed." NBC News. August 20, 2024. NBC Universal. https://www.nbcnews.com/news/us-news/derek-chauvin-ex-officer-convicted-murdering-george-floyd-moved-new-pr-rcna167437

The Canadian Press. "Quebec College of Physicians sends out warning about woman pretending to be a doctor." Global News. Corus Entertainment Inc. June 2, 2021. https://globalnews.ca/news/7915442/quebec-fake-doctor-college-warning/

The Canadian Press. "UBC regrets handling of Mary Ellen Turpel-Lafond case, as she loses honour at different university." Vancouver Sun. Postmedia Network Inc. January 18, 2023. https://vancouversun.com/news/local-news/ubc-regrets-handling-mary-ellen-turpel-lafond

Urquhart, Catherine. "Coquitlam Mounties coule face dismissal over shocking group chat." Global News. September 20, 2024. https://globalnews.ca/news/10766644/coqutialm-rcmp-group-chat-allegations/VantageScore. "The Complete Guide to Your VantageScore." October 11, 2019. https://www.vantage-score.com/the-complete-guide-to-your-vantagescore/

Wolford, Ben. "What is GDPR, the EU's new data protection law?" GRPR.EU. Accessed September 13, 2024. https://gdpr.eu/what-is-gdpr/

Yang, John, Kaisha Young and Claire Mufson. "What's changed in Minneapolis four years after George Floyd's death." PBS News. NewsHour Productions LLC. May 25, 2024. https://www.pbs.org/newshour/show/whats-changed-in-minneapolis-four-years-after-george-floyds-death

Zurkowsky, Herb. "CF Montréal terminates Sandro Grande one day after coach was hired." Montreal Gazette. Postmedia Network Inc. January 11, 2023. https://montrealgazette.com/sports/soccer/mls/club-de-foot-montreal/pq-denounces-cf-montreal-hiring-of-sandro-grande

Other Titles from Ingenium Books

In the Thick of It:
Mastering the Art of Leading
from the Middle

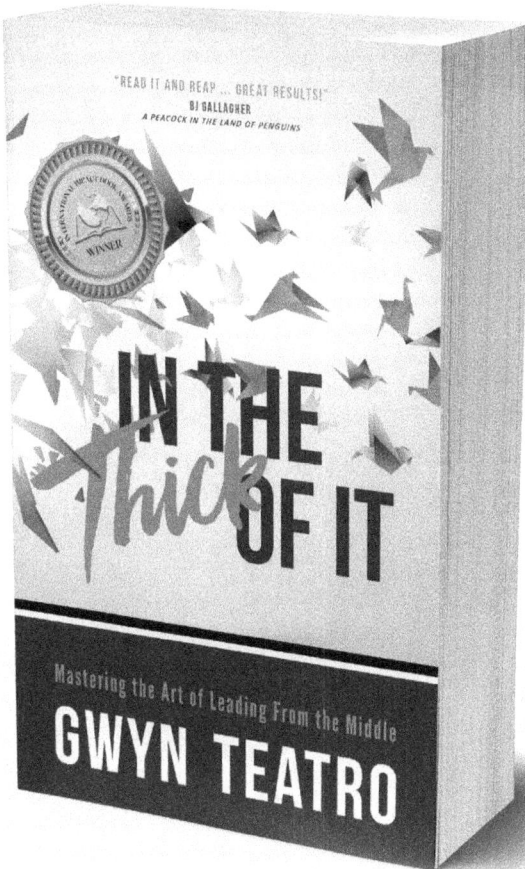

ingeniumbooks.com/ITTOI

Just Do You:
Authenticity, Leadership, and Your Personal Brand

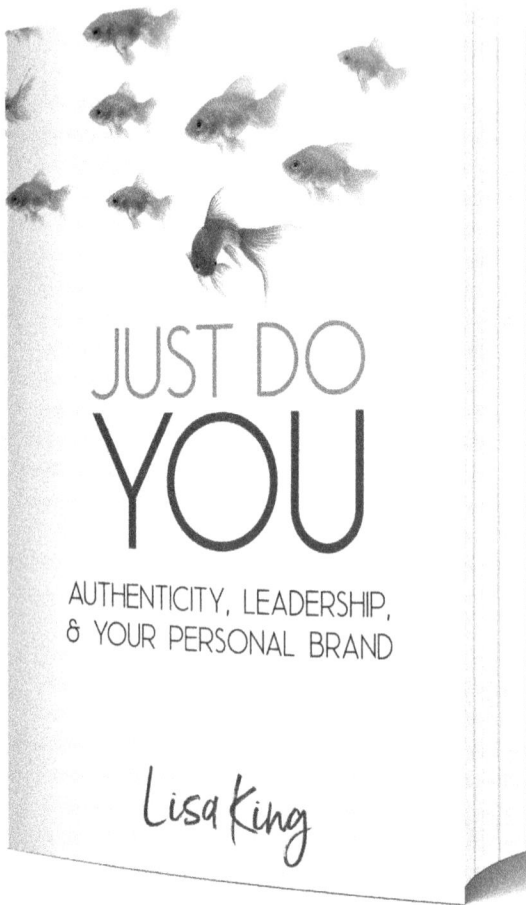

ingeniumbooks.com/justdoyou

Chill:
The Wine Lover's
Introduction to Cannabis

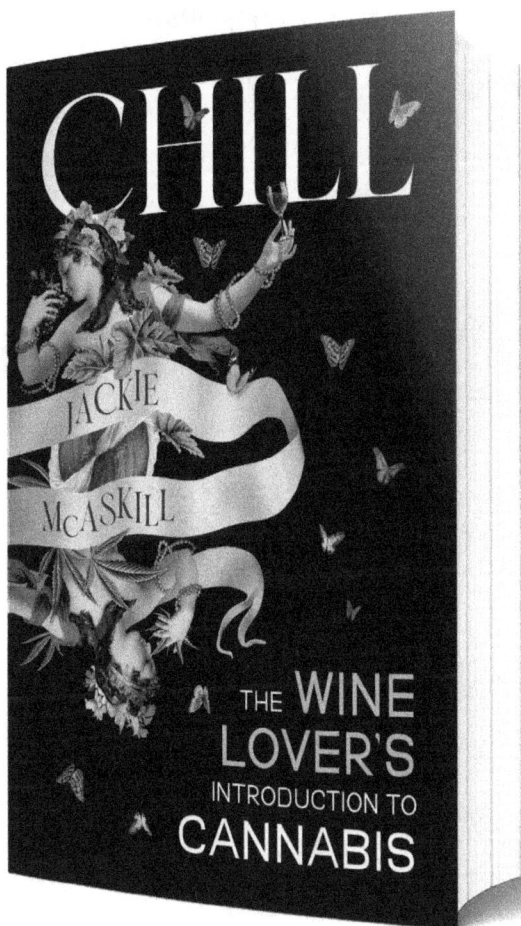

ingeniumbooks.com/CHILL

12 Elephants and a Dragon:
A Memoir of Survival
and the Kindness of Strangers

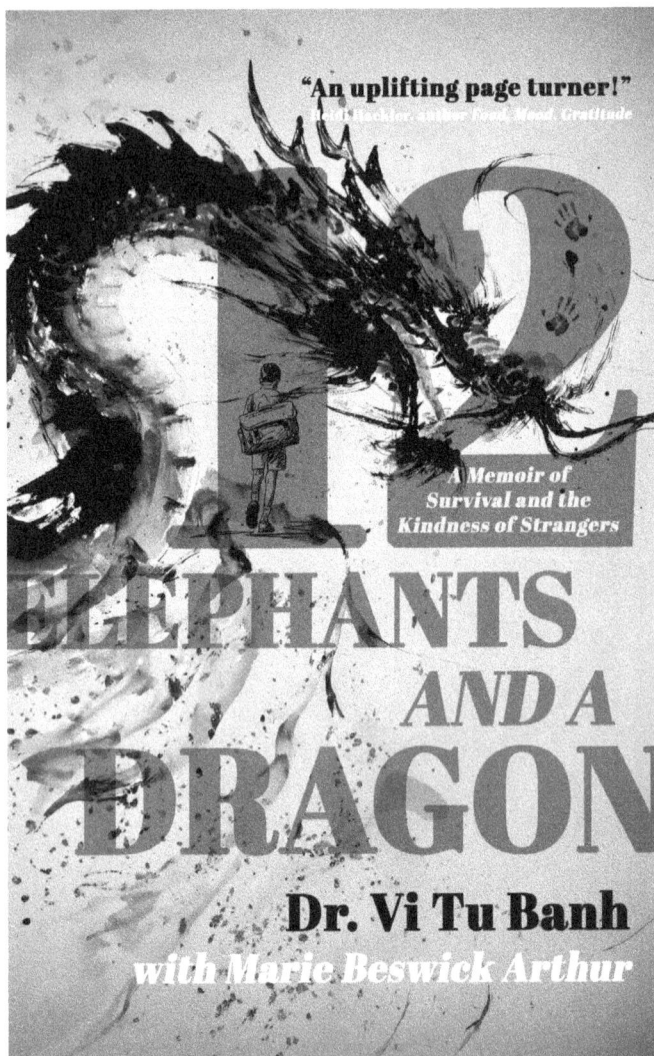

"An uplifting page turner!"
Heidi Hackler, author *Food, Mood, Gratitude*

12

A Memoir of
Survival and the
Kindness of Strangers

ELEPHANTS
AND A
DRAGON

Dr. Vi Tu Banh
with Marie Beswick Arthur

ingeniumbooks.com/12ED

The Tortured Traveller:
How I Survived
the Worst... Vacation... Ever

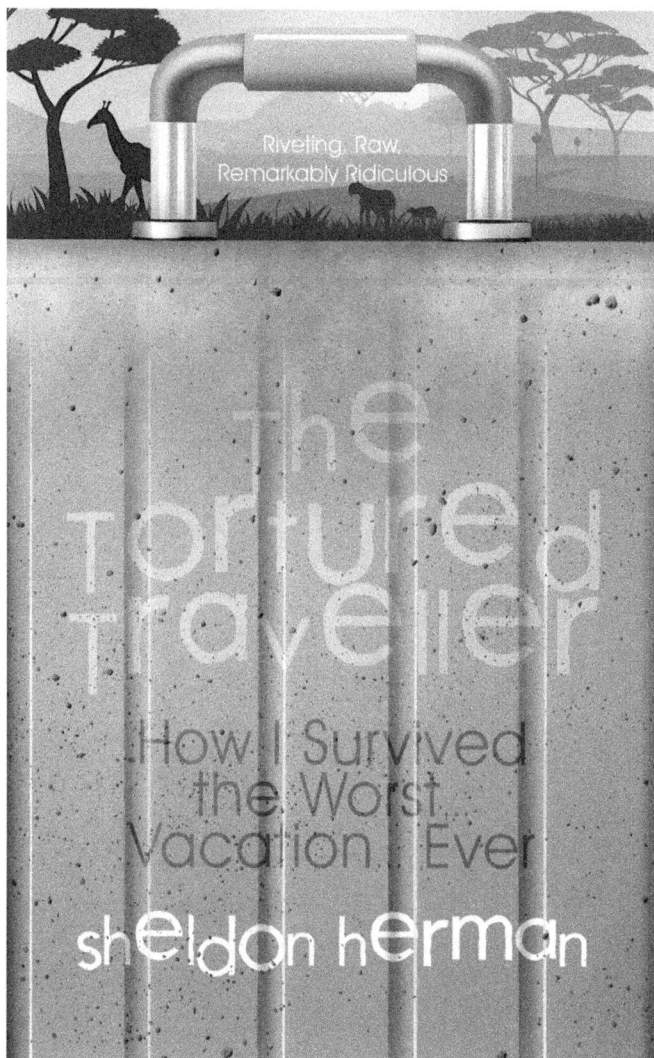

Riveting. Raw.
Remarkably Ridiculous

the
Tortured
Traveller

How I Survived
the Worst...
Vacation... Ever

sheldon herman

ingeniumbooks.com/TORT

Mom on Wheels:
The Power of Purpose
for a Parent with Paraplegia

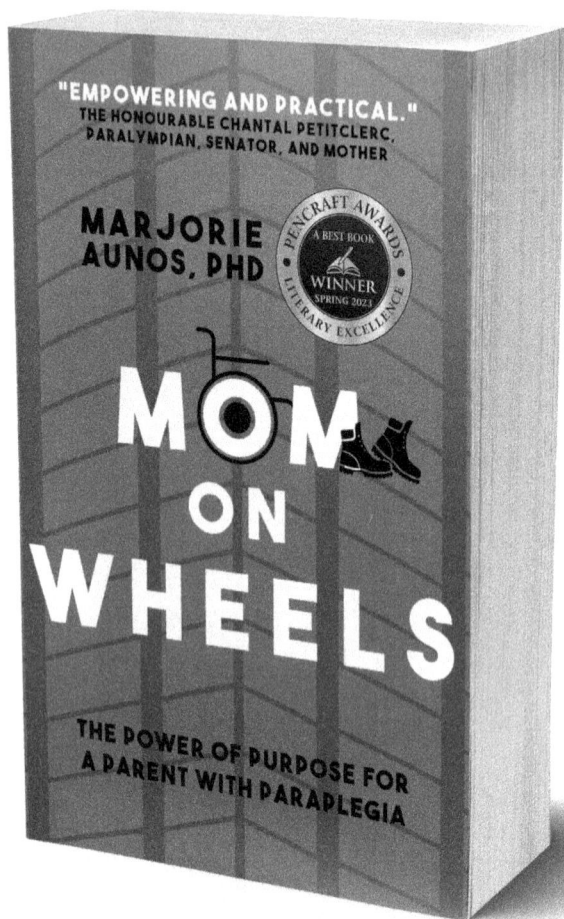

"EMPOWERING AND PRACTICAL."
THE HONOURABLE CHANTAL PETITCLERC,
PARALYMPIAN, SENATOR, AND MOTHER

MARJORIE
AUNOS, PHD

PENCRAFT AWARDS
A BEST BOOK
WINNER
SPRING 2023
LITERARY EXCELLENCE

MOM
ON
WHEELS

THE POWER OF PURPOSE FOR
A PARENT WITH PARAPLEGIA

ingeniumbooks.com/as3o

The Promise of Psychedelics:
Science Based Hope
for Better Mental Health

THE **PROMISE** OF
PSYCHEDELICS

DR. PETER
SILVERSTONE

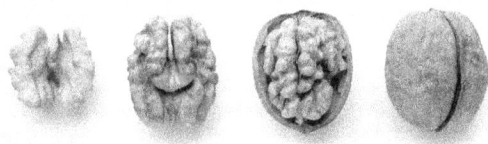

Science-Based Hope
for Better Mental Health

ingeniumbooks.com/0ugf

Choices:
How to Mend or End
a Broken Relationship

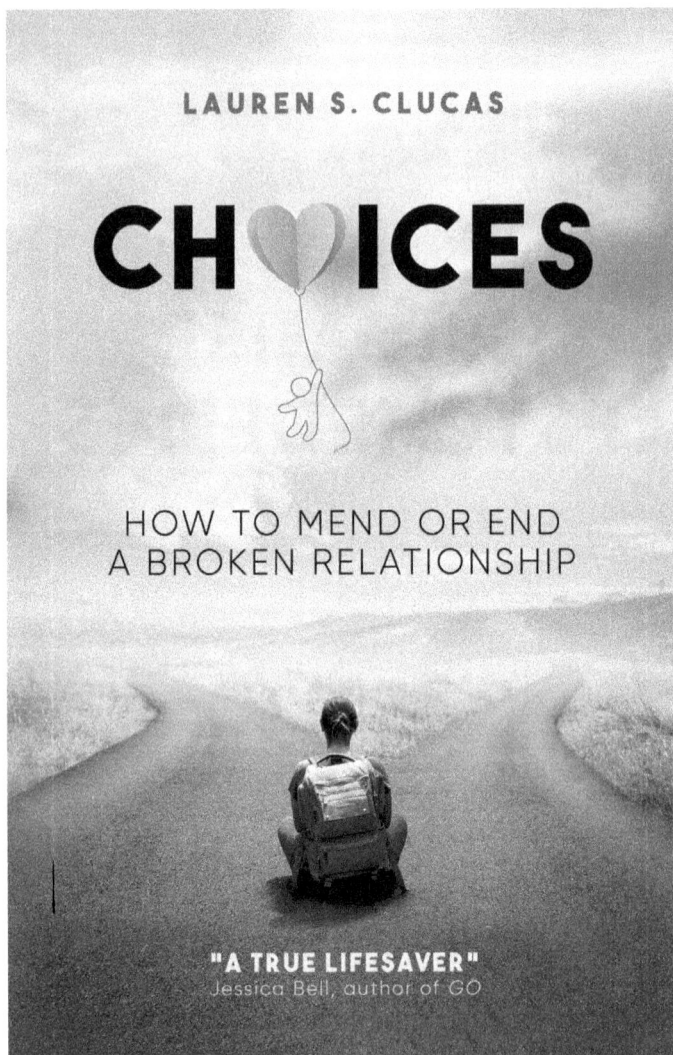

LAUREN S. CLUCAS

CH♥ICES

HOW TO MEND OR END
A BROKEN RELATIONSHIP

"A TRUE LIFESAVER"
Jessica Bell, author of GO

ingeniumbooks.com/CHCS

Choices:
Workbook

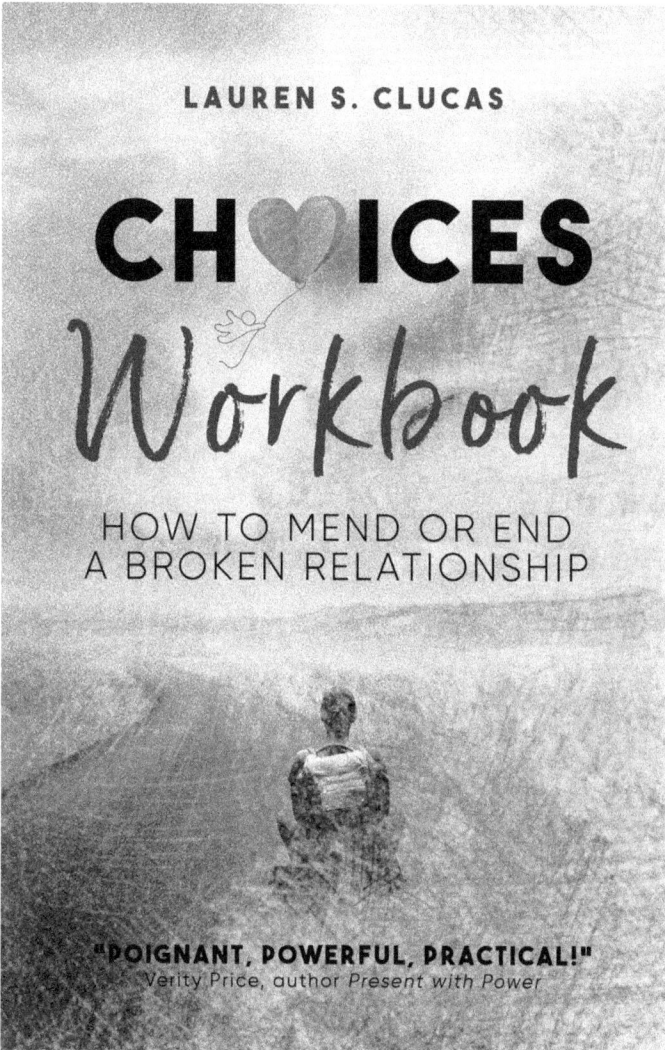

LAUREN S. CLUCAS

CH♥ICES
Workbook

HOW TO MEND OR END
A BROKEN RELATIONSHIP

"POIGNANT, POWERFUL, PRACTICAL!"
Verity Price, author *Present with Power*

ingeniumbooks.com/CHWKBK

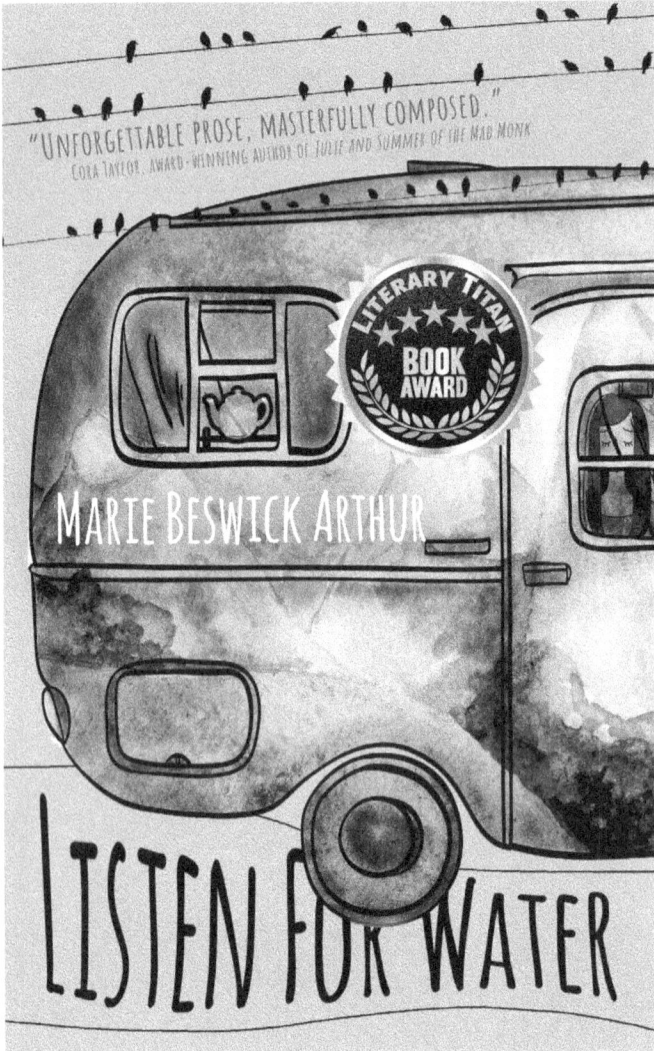

"UNFORGETTABLE PROSE, MASTERFULLY COMPOSED."
CORA TAYLOR, AWARD-WINNING AUTHOR OF JULIE AND SUMMER OF THE MAD MONK

LITERARY TITAN
BOOK AWARD

MARIE BESWICK ARTHUR

LISTEN FOR WATER

Four Fridays with Christina:
Friendship, Death, and
Lessons Learned by Letting Go

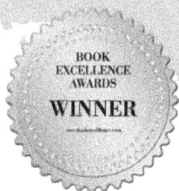

BOOK EXCELLENCE AWARDS WINNER

Cynthia Barlow

four
fridays
with christina

FRIENDSHIP, DEATH, AND LESSONS
LEARNED BY *Letting Go*

"an unforgettable
journey of illumination"
Terri Cheney, author of
New York Times bestseller
Manic: A Memoir

ingeniumbooks.com/FFEB

www.ingramcontent.com/pod-product-compliance
Lightning Source LLC
Chambersburg PA
CBHW030511210326
41597CB00013B/873